SpringerBriefs in Electrical and Computer Engineering

For further volumes:
http://www.springer.com/series/10059

Sandeep Kumar

Agent-Based Semantic Web Service Composition

 Springer

Sandeep Kumar
Department of Electronics and Computer Engineering
Indian Institute of Technology Roorkee
Roorkee
India

ISSN 2191-8112   ISSN 2191-8120   (electronic)
ISBN 978-1-4614-4662-0   ISBN 978-1-4614-4663-7   (eBook)
DOI 10.1007/978-1-4614-4663-7
Springer New York Heidelberg Dordrecht London

Library of Congress Control Number: 2012942927

Printed on acid-free paper

Springer is part of Springer Science+Business Media (www.springer.com)

Preface

The basic aim of the Semantic Web is to create a layer on the existing Web enabling advanced automatic processing of the web-content that further allows the sharing and processing of data by both humans and software. Semantic Web Services can be defined as the self-sufficient, reusable software components that can be used to fulfill a particular task. In the real-life scenario, the client requirements cannot be satisfied using only the single service component. In such cases, service discovery and selection is used for selecting the most appropriate service components followed by the service composition for generating the aggregation of selected service components according to the requested task. Different types of approaches providing Semantic Web service composition are available in the literature. In this book, we are mainly concerned with the agent-based Semantic Web service composition. Multiagent-based Semantic Web service composition is based upon the argument that a multiagent system can be considered as a service composition system, in which different involved agents represent the different individual services. The service is considered as an intelligent agent capability implemented as a self-contained software component. The book has been organized as follows. Chapter 1 provides a brief introduction to some of the basic topics related to Semantic Web such as Web, Semantic Web services, Semantic Web service composition, ontology etc. In Chap. 2, a general introduction to the terms agents, multiagent systems, and negotiation has been given. Chapter 3 discusses the basics of agent-based service composition. An overview of some of the multiagent-based Semantic Web service composition approaches available in the literature has also been given. The chapter also presents models for agent-based Semantic Web service composition basically varying on the use of a coordinator agent in the composition process. A brief overview of a service selection model providing formalization of various Quality of Service (QoS) parameters and cognitive parameters of agent for selecting the most appropriate service provider agent has also been presented. In Chap. 4, initially a brief discussion of the multi-attribute negotiation and an overview of some of the available multi-attribute negotiation approaches has been given. An agent-based, utility-based, multi-attribute negotiation approach providing negotiation between semantic Web services has been described in detail. Finally, in Chap. 5, we have proposed a negotiation-agreements-based Semantic Web service selection and composition approach. A mathematical model providing multi-attribute negotiation-based service selection using evaluation of negotiation-agreements has also been proposed. I am hopeful that the book will not only provide a good introductory reference but will also give the reader a breadth and depth of this topic. All feedbacks are welcome at sandeepkumargarg@gmail.com.

Roorkee, India, April 2012   Sandeep Kumar

Acknowledgments

I would like to express my sincere thanks to Prof. R. B. Mishra of the Department of Computer Engineering, Indian Institute of Technology, Banaras Hindu University (India) for contributing in the last chapter of the book and also guiding and encouraging me throughout the writing of this book. I am also thankful to the faculty members of the Department of Electronics and Computer Engineering, Indian Institute of Technology Roorkee (India), for their constant support and encouragement. I am also grateful to the editor and the publication team of Springer. Last but not least, I am thankful to the almighty God, my teachers, and my family members without whose love, nurture, and support I could never have accomplished this project. I am really thankful to my parents, my sisters, my wife Ankita, my daughter Aastha, and my brother Kuldeep. I have no words to mention the support, patience, and sacrifice of my wife and my parents. I dedicate this book to God and to my family.

Sandeep Kumar

Contents

Chapter 1
Introduction

Abstract Semantic Web is the extension of current Web in which information is given well defined meaning better enabling computer and people to work in cooperation. It has a layered architecture. Various layers in the architecture follow the principles of downward compatibility and upward partial understanding. Among others, some of the Semantic Web languages are RDF, RDF-S, DAML-ONT (DARPA Agent Markup Language—Ontology), OIL (Ontology Inference Layer), DAML + OIL, OWL (Web Ontology Language), DAML-S, and OWL-S. Semantic web services can be obtained from the augmentation of web service through semantic annotations. Various services related processes are service discovery, selection, composition, invocation and monitoring. In this chapter, a very brief introduction of some of the basic topics related to Semantic Web has been given.

Keywords Semantic Web · Semantic Web Languages · Ontology · Service composition

1.1 Semantic Web

Finding the right piece of information on the Web is generally a nightmare. While searching the Web for some specific information, one gets lost into the huge amount of irrelevant materials and may often miss the relevant matter. Searches are often imprecise and returns pointers to many thousands of pages. User must read through the retrieved documents to extract the desired information (Fensel et al. 2005). The current search-engines do not seem to be 'information retriever' but only the 'location finder' (Antoniou and Harmelen 2004). The main reason behind these problems is that the meaning of the web-content is not machine-accessible. Current

S. Kumar, *Agent-Based Semantic Web Service Composition*,
SpringerBriefs in Electrical and Computer Engineering,
DOI: 10.1007/978-1-4614-4663-7_1, © The Author(s) 2012

softwares have very limited capabilities in interpreting the sentences and extracting useful information for users. One solution to this problem is to represent web-content in a form that is more easily machine-processable and using intelligent techniques over these representations. This plan of revolutionizing the World Wide Web is called as Semantic Web initiative (Antoniou and Harmelen 2004).

The Semantic Web is not a separate Web. It is an extension of the current one, in which information is given well-defined meaning, better enabling computers and people to work in cooperation (Berners-Lee 2001). Its basic aim is to create a layer on the existing Web that enables advanced automatic processing of the web-contents so that data can be shared and processed by both humans and software. The Semantic Web uses the concept of self-describing, machine-readable knowledge, which is accessible using standard web-programming constructs. Semantic layer connects the different knowledge-sources having explicit and defined semantics, across the Web (Schwartz 2003). Semantic Web aims at offering a solution, capturing and exploiting the meaning of terms to transform current Web from information-presentation platform to a platform that focuses on understanding and reasoning with the information (McGuinness et al. 2002). Semantic Web technology will enable structural and semantic definitions of documents providing completely new possibilities. It will enable intelligent search instead of keyword matching, query answering instead of information retrieval, document exchange among departments via ontology mappings, and definition of customized views on documents (Fensel et al. 2005). As the research in Semantic Web is still to its infancy, so a lot of areas in Semantic Web are there which need researchers' attention such as infrastructure, languages, resources, applications, Semantic Web Services (SWSs) and related processes like discovery, selection, composition, monitoring etc. and others (Euzenat 2002).

1.2 Web Versus Semantic Web

In this section, some of the basic properties of the existing Web are compared with the Semantic Web. Table 1.1 shows the summary of comparison.

1.3 Layered Architecture of Semantic Web

Semantic Web has a layered architecture (Berners-Lee 2000). Various layers in the Semantic Web architecture follow the principles of downward compatibility and upward partial understanding. The layered architecture presented here is the initial basic layered architecture of Semantic Web (Berners-Lee 2000) proposed in support of the founding vision of the Semantic Web (Berners-Lee et al. 2001). The main layers of Semantic Web design and vision is shown in Fig. 1.1 (Berners-Lee 2000).

Table 1.1 The web versus the semantic web

Current Web	Semantic Web
Currently, the contents on the Web are machine readable, these are not machine processable	The contents on the Semantic Web should be machine-readable as well as machine understandable (Berners-Lee et al. 2001)
Current web is just like a book, having multiple hyperlinked documents	Data is given well-defined meaning such that it is understandable by machines (Berners-Lee et al. 2001)
Current web have only visual design and shared functional languages and hence does not allow any existing knowledge representation system to be exported onto the Web	The Semantic Web is to provide a language expressing the data that can be used for reasoning about the data. It should also allow rules making any existing knowledge representation system to be exported onto the web (Floridi 2009)
Current web is called a web of documents containing data	Semantic web is the web of ontologies having data with formal meaning (Berners-Lee et al. 2001)
Resource utilization is minimum i. e. web resources are not annotated properly by the metadata	Resource utilization is maximum i. e. web resources are annotated properly by the metadata
It has been determined that inaccessible part of the web is about five hundred times more than what search engines find (Sherman and Price 2001)	In Semantic Web, formal semantics of data is available via ontologies and hence completely accessible to semantic search engines
The information searching, accessing, extracting, interpreting and processing from the current web is difficult and time consuming	The information searching, accessing, extracting, interpreting and processing from the Semantic Web is easy and efficient (Berners-Lee et al. 2001)

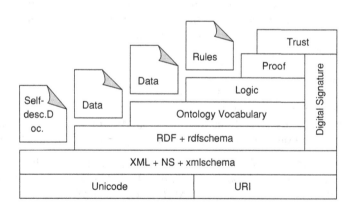

Fig. 1.1 Layered semantic web architecture (Berners-Lee 2000)

The bottom layer includes XML (Extensible Mark-up Language) that can be used to write structured web-documents with user-defined vocabulary. It is particularly useful for sending documents across the Web.

The next layer is composed of RDF (Resource Description Framework) and RDF-Schema (RDF-S). RDF is a basic data model for writing simple statements about web resources (Antoniou and Harmelen 2004). In RDF, entities are represented using unique identifiers and statements valid between the entities. A statement connects a subject i.e. source entity, and an object i.e. destination entity, via a predicate/property. Altogether, an RDF description is a list of triples: a subject, a predicate, an object. RDF-S can be considered as a primitive language for writing the ontologies. RDF-Schema (RDF-S) uses RDF for defining additional constructs useful for creating object-oriented schemas in a separate namespace.

The next layer is composed of ontology vocabulary representing more powerful ontology languages expanding RDF-S and capable of representing more complex relationships between web-objects. A lot of ontological languages such as DAML-ONT (DARPA Agent Markup Language—Ontology), OIL (Ontology Inference Layer), DAML + OIL, OWL (Web Ontology Language), DAML-S, and OWL-S have been developed. These languages specifically work on the Web for describing web contents in machine-processable form. In actual practice, these languages are extension of RDF with formal rigor of description logic and ontological primitives. OWL-S is the recent ontological language that can be used for describing the web-contents. DAML-ONT is the first ontology-based language. It was launched by DARPA (Defense Advanced Research Projects Agency) in 2000. DAML is the first programming language that instead of using human-interpretation uses agents and programs for interpretation and reasoning of web-contents (McGuinness et al. 2002). OIL was developed by European Project Ontobroker. This language has an inference layer of ontologies with modeling primitives from frame-based languages and formal foundations of description logic. It supports the formal semantics as well as various reasoning services provided by description logic (Payne and Tamma 2005). DAML + OIL has best of the features of both DAML-ONT and OIL. DAML + OIL provides various features as below (McGuinness et al. 2002):

• Describing classes
• Describing individual instance using subclasses
• Describing properties of objects
• Providing cardinality restrictions over the properties of classes & subclasses
• Providing restriction over of the type of property of classes & subclasses

OWL is the successor of DAML + OIL language. It has the ability of writing the ontologies which can support description logic-based reasoners (Horrocks 2005). DAML-S is the successor of DAML + OIL and OWL. It considers the system in the form of different services and can write ontologies organized in three parts: Profile, Model, and Grounding (Martin 2002). OWL-S has its basis on OWL. It can be used to describe the semantically rich characteristics of services on the Web. OWL-S is organized in four parts named Profile, Process model, Grounding, and Services (Martin 2003). The details on some of the Semantic Web languages can be referred from RDF (Resource Description Framework) (Herman et al.

2008), DAML (DARPA Agent Mark-up Language) (DARPA 2008), OWL (Web Ontology Language) (McGuinness and Harmelen 2004) etc.

The logic layer represents the further enhancement of ontology languages to allow the writing of application-specific declarative knowledge. The actual deductive process as well as the representation of proofs in web-languages from lower layer and proof validation is involved in the next layer. From the use of digital signatures and other kind of knowledge based upon the recommendations or rating of trusted agent and certification agencies, the trust layer is emerged. It is located at the top of pyramid to show that trust is a high-level and crucial concept. Web can achieve its full potential only if the users have trust in its operations and the quality of information provided by it (Antoniou and Harmelen 2004).

Apart from the first Semantic Web layered architecture (Berners-Lee 2000) described above, Tim Berners-Lee has proposed other versions of layered architectures. Second version is available in (Berners-Lee 2003). Third version is available in (Berners-Lee 2005) and fourth version of the layered architecture can be referred from (Berners-Lee 2006).

1.4 Semantic Web Service

Semantic Web Services (SWS) can be defined as the self-sufficient, reusable software components that can be used to fulfill a particular task. These services generally have modular structure and can be published and invoked through the Web. As described in (Payne and Lassila 2004), SWSs are developed through the augmentation of web service descriptions through Semantic Web annotations and hence facilitating the higher automation of service discovery, service composition, service invocation, and service monitoring in an open, unregulated, and often chaotic environment i.e. Web (Payne and Lassila 2004). SWSs can be developed by creating semantic mark-up of web services to make them computer-interpretable, user-apparent, and agent-ready. Figure 1.2 shows the emergence of SWSs.

Various usage processes for the SWSs are publication, discovery, selection, composition, mediation, and execution (Kappel et al. 2006) as defined below:

- Publication is the process of making available the description of capabilities of a service, various parameters associated with it, and functionalities it has to offer to the outside world.
- Discovery is the process of automatically locating the different web services providing a particular service and suitable for a given task.
- Service selection is the process that involves choosing the most appropriate service for a given task from the discovered candidate services.
- Service composition is the process of aggregation of existing atomic services to generate a composite service that can satisfy the ultimate goal. In most of cases, Semantic Web based systems can not satisfy the client requirements using only

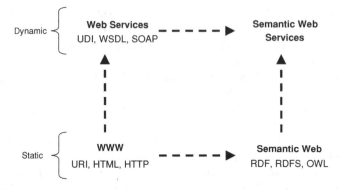

Fig. 1.2 Web, web services, semantic web, and semantic web services (Fensel et al. 2002)

the single service component. Then, the service composition is used to combine the services for achieving a specified goal.

- Mediation is used to solve the possible semantic mismatches at data-level, protocol-level, and at the process-level.
- Invocation of services is the process that is performed during the execution process.

1.5 Semantic Web Service Composition

Semantic Web service composition is the process of generating the aggregated service by the integration of independent available component services for satisfying a client-request that cannot be satisfied by any available single service. In the Semantic Web based systems, some of the SWSs related processes are service publication, service discovery, service selection, service composition, service mediation, and execution (Kappel et al. 2006). Among these processes, the process of SWS composition can be considered as one of the most important process for achieving the high-level goal of satisfying the user's request. In most of the cases, the Semantic Web based systems can not satisfy the client-requirements using only the single available service component. In that scenario, service discovery and further the service selection is used for selecting the most appropriate service components followed by the service composition for generating the aggregation of selected service components according to the requested task. SWS composition increases the capability of an application to satisfy user's requests by theoretically generating an unlimited number of new services from the composition of limited service-components (Kumar and Mishra 2009). In the literature, various types of approaches for SWS composition are available such as ontology-driven, agent-based, context-based, iterative, BPEL4WS based, template-based, logic-based, AI (Artificial Intelligence) planning-based, workflow-driven etc. Currently in the case of Web, to satisfy the user-request if some task requires composition of web services that need to interoperate, then following activities need to be performed:

- User selects the participating web services.
- Manually specify the composition.
- User ensures that any software for interoperation is custom-created.
- User provides the input at choice-points.

The semantic mark-up of web services can enable automation of this composition process by encoding the information necessary to select, compose, and respond to services at the service websites (Kappel et al. 2006). The service composition process can involve composition of homogeneous as well as heterogeneous services. The interface, properties, and capabilities of the SWSs are encoded in a machine-understandable form to allow an easy integration of heterogeneous SWSs (Kumar and Mishra 2008).

1.6 Ontology

An ontology is a formal, explicit specification of a shared conceptualization. In this definition, 'Formal' means that the ontology should be machine understandable, 'Explicit' means that the type of concepts used and the constraints on their use are explicitly defined, 'Shared' refers to the notion that an ontology is not restricted to some individual but accepted by a group, and the 'Conceptualization' refers to an abstract model of some phenomenon in the world that identifies the relevant concepts of that phenomenon (Gruber 1993). An ontology defines a set of representational primitives with which to model a domain of knowledge. Various representational primitives include classes or sets, attributes or properties, and relations among class members (Gruber 2008). In the context of Web, ontologies provide a shared understanding of a domain. This will enable to overcome the differences in terminology on the Web. Thus, ontologies can be used to provide semantic interoperability (Antoniou and Harmelen 2004). Some formal languages can be used to encode the ontologies called as ontology languages. In the technology stack of Semantic Web standards (Berners-Lee et al. 2001), ontologies are called out as an explicit layer (Gruber 2008). Some of the important ontology languages for the Web are: RDF, RDF-S, OWL, OWL-S etc.

References

G. Antoniou, Harmelen F.v, *A Semantic Web Primer* (The MIT Press, Cambridge 2004)
T. Berners-Lee, Semantic web—XML, 2000 (2000). W3C Website, http://www.w3.org/2000/Talks/1206-xml2k-tbl/slide10-0.html. Accessed 11 Aug 2006

T. Berners-Lee, The semantic web and challenges (2003). W3C Website, http://www.w3.org/
2003/Talks/01-sweb-tbl/Overview.html. Accessed 10 Oct 2006

T. Berners-Lee, WWW2005 Keynote (2005). W3C Website, http://www.w3.org/2005/Talks/
0511-keynote-tbl/. Accessed 10 Oct 2006

T. Berners-Lee, Artificial intelligence and the semantic web: AAAI2006 Keynote (2006). W3C
Website, http://www.w3.org/2006/Talks/0718-aaai-tbl/Overview.html. Accessed 12 Oct 2006

T. Berners-Lee, J. Hendler, O. Lassila, The semantic web, scientific American magazine (2001).
http://www.scientificamerican.com/article.cfm?id=the-semanticweb. May 2001, pp. 1–7

DARPA (2008) The DARPA agent mark-up language. DAML Website, http://www.daml.org/.
Accessed 28 Feb 2008

J. Euzenat, Research challenges and perspectives of the semantic web. IEEE Intell. Syst. **17**(5),
86–88 (2002)

D. Fensel, C. Bussler, A. Maedche, Semantic Web Enabled Web Services. in *Proceedings of the
First International Semantic Web Conference on The Semantic Web*, 09–12 June 2002

D. Fensel, J. Hendler, H. Lieberman, W. Wahlster, *Spinning the Semantic Web* (The MIT Press,
Cambridge, 2005)

L. Floridi, Web2.0 vs. the semantic web: a philosophical assessment. Episteme J. **6**(1), 25–37
(2009)

T.R. Gruber, A translation approach to portable ontology specifications, Knowl. Acquis. J. **5**(2),
199–220 (1993)

T. Gruber, Ontology, the Encyclopedia of Database Systems, ed. by L. Liu, M. Tamer Özsu,
Springer-Verlag (2008) http://www.springerreference.com/docs/html/chapterdbid/64216.html

I. Herman, R. Swick, D. Brickley, Resource Description Framework (RDF) (2008). W3C
Website, http://www.w3.org/RDF/. Accessed 28 Feb 2008

I. Horrocks, *Description Logics in Ontology Applications*, ed. by B. Beckert. In Proceedings of
the 9th Intternational Conference on Automated Reasoning with Analytic Tableaux and
Related Methods (TABLEAUX 2005). Lecture Notes in Artificial Intelligence, vol. 3702
(Springer, Berlin, 2005), pp. 2–13

G. Kappel, B. Pröll, S. Reich, W. Retschitzegger, *Web Engineering* (Wiley, Hoboken, 2006)

S. Kumar, R.B. Mishra, A framework towards semantic web service composition based on multi-
agent system. Int. J. Inf. Technol. Web Eng. IGI USA **3**(4), 59–81 (2008)

S. Kumar, R.B. Mishra, Towards a framework for classification and recommendation of semantic
web service composition approaches. Int. J. Comput. Appl. **31**(4), 274–281 (2009)

D. Martin, DAML-S: semantic markup for web services. The DAML services coalition (2002).
http://www.daml.org/services/daml-s/0.7/daml-s.html#foot27. Accessed 16 June 2009

D. Martin, OWL-S: semantic markup for web services. The OWL services coalition (2003).
http://www.daml.org/services/owl-s/1.0/owl-s.html. Accessed 16 June 2009

D.L. McGuinness, R. Fikes, J. Hendler, L.A. Stein, DAML + OIL: an ontology language for the
semantic web. IEEE Intell. Syst. **17**(5), 72–80 (2002)

D.L. McGuinness, F.V. Harmelen, OWL Web Ontology Language Overview (2004). W3C
Recommendations 2004, W3C Website, http://www.w3.org/TR/owl-features/. Accessed 13
Feb 2008

T. Payne, O. Lassila, Semantic web services. IEEE Intell. Syst. **19**(4), 14–15 (2004)

T. Payne, V. Tamma, Towards semantic web agents: knowledge web and AgentLink. Knowl.
Eng. Rev. **20**(2), 191–196 (2005)

D.G. Schwartz, From open is semantics to the semantic web: the road ahead. IEEE Intell. Syst.
18(3), 52–58 (2003)

C. Sherman, G. Price, *The Invisible Web: Uncovering Information Sources Search Engines Can't
See* (CyberAge Books, Medford, 2001)

Chapter 2
Semantic Web Agents

Abstract Agent denotes the piece of software that possesses the properties of autonomy, social ability, reactivity, proactivity, temporal continuity, and goal-orientedness. Multi-agent system consists of a number of agents which are capable of interacting with each other. In these systems, the agents are capable to cooperate, coordinate, and negotiate with each other. Various activities in the Semantic Web based systems are performed by Semantic Web agents. The inter-agent dependencies among these agents are managed using the process of negotiation. Negotiation is the process by which a group of agents come to a mutually acceptable agreement on some matter. In this chapter, a general introduction to the terms agents, multi-agent systems and negotiation has been given.

Keywords Agents · Multi-agent systems · Negotiation

2.1 Semantic Web Agents

Although there is no universally accepted definition of the term Agent (Wooldridge 2002), there are some of the similar definitions available in the literature. As per (Wooldridge 2002), an agent is a computer system that is situated in some environment and that is capable of some autonomous action in this environment in order to meet its design objective. An agent basically has two important capabilities. Firstly, agents are capable of autonomous action to some extent and hence are capable of deciding for themselves what they need to do in order to satisfy their deign objectives. Secondly, agents are capable of interacting with other agents by exchanging data and they can engage with other agents in some social activities such as coordination, cooperation, negotiation etc. According to (Antoniou and Harmelen 2004), agent is a piece of software that

S. Kumar, *Agent-Based Semantic Web Service Composition*,
SpringerBriefs in Electrical and Computer Engineering,
DOI: 10.1007/978-1-4614-4663-7_2, © The Author(s) 2012

works autonomously and proactively. Agent denotes a software-based computer system that has following properties (Wooldridge 2002; Kappel et al. 2006):

- Autonomy: operates without direct intervention of human and having self-control over its actions and internal states.
- Social ability: has ability to interact with other agents and humans using some agent communication language.
- Reactivity: has ability to perceive its environment and respond in timely fashion to the occurring changes.
- Proactivity: exhibition of goal-directed behavior by taking initiative.
- Temporal continuity: continuously running process either in active or in sleeping state in background.
- Goal orientedness: capable of handling complex and high-level tasks by taking decision on how much a task is best split into smaller sub-tasks and in which order and in what way these sub-tasks need to be performed.

Among others, some of the activities performed by the Semantic Web agent are (Antoniou and Harmelen 2004):

- Receiving some tasks and preferences from the service requester.
- Seeking information from the Web sources.
- Communicating with other agents.
- Comparing information about user requirements and preferences.
- Selecting certain choices.
- Giving answer to the service requester or user.

Some of the technologies used by Semantic Web agent are (Antoniou and Harmelen 2004):

- *Ontologies* are used to assist in Web searches. These are also used to interpret the retrieved information and to communicate with other agents. It uses meta-data for identifying and extracting information from Web sources.
- *Logic* is used for processing of retrieved information and drawing a conclusion.
- *Agent communication languages* are used for communicating with other agents.
- *Formal representation* is needed for representing the cognitive parameters such as belief, desire, intention etc. of agents.
- *Negotiation* is the process by which a group of agents reach to a mutually acceptable agreement on some matter such as price, quality etc. It is the process of making a joint decision by two or more parties (Jennings et al. 2001). In general, before selecting a certain agent for taking its service, the requester agent negotiate with it over various service parameters such as price, quality etc. to reach at a mutually acceptable agreement.

2.2 Multi-Agent Systems

As the technology matures and addresses increasingly complex applications, the need for systems that consist of multiple agents that communicate in a peer-to-peer fashion is becoming apparent (Sycara 1998). Multi-agent systems are systems composed of multiple interacting computing elements known as agents. Multi-agent system consists of a number of agents which are capable of interacting with each other by exchanging messages through some computer network infrastructure. In these systems, mostly the agents are acting on behalf of users and are having very different goals and motivations. They are capable to cooperate, coordinate and negotiate with each other (Wooldridge 2002). Following are some of the characteristics of multi-agent systems (Sycara 1998):

- Each agent has incomplete information or capabilities for solving the problem. Thus, it has a limited viewpoint.
- There is no system global control.
- Data are decentralized.
- Computation is asynchronous.

Multi-agent system technology is capable of enhancing the performance of systems along the following dimensions (Sycara 1998):

- *Computational efficiency.* These systems exploit the concurrency of computation and communication is kept minimal.
- *Reliability.* These systems provide graceful recovery of component failures. As agents with redundant capabilities or appropriate inter-agent coordination are found dynamically.
- *Extensibility.* As the number and the capabilities of agents working on a problem can be altered.
- *Robustness.* These systems are capable of tolerating uncertainty.
- *Maintainability.* Multi-agent system is easier to maintain because of its modularity.
- *Responsiveness.* Due to its modular nature, these systems can handle anomalies locally.
- *Flexibility.* Agents with different abilities can adaptively organize to solve the problem.
- *Reuse.* Functionally specific agents can be reused in different agent teams.

2.3 Negotiation

Negotiation is a form of decision-making where two or more parties jointly search a space of possible solutions with the goal of reaching a consensus (Rosenschein and Zlotkin 1994). Negotiation is the process by which a group of agents come to a mutually acceptable agreement on some matter. In this process, agents first verbalize demands and then move toward an agreement through a process of concession formation or search for new alternatives (Muller 1996; Zhang et al. 2005). There are mainly three approaches to the automated negotiation i.e. Game theoretic approach, Heuristic approach, and Argumentation-based approach (Jennings et al. 2001). Multi-agent systems can have either competitive behavior or cooperative behavior. In the competitive behavior, the participating agents are self interested and their activities may be conflicting with the activities of other agents. In cooperative environment, the activities of agents are such that they are mutually cooperating each other to reach the final goal. Negotiation is required in both of these environments. So, negotiation in multi-agent systems can be either competitive negotiation or cooperative negotiation. In competitive negotiation, the agents are self-interested and each one tries to maximize its local utility. In cooperative negotiation, the agents try to maximize their global utility. There can be different degree of cooperation in the cooperative negotiation. The two extremes are: global cooperation and local cooperation. In global cooperation, an agent, while making its local decision, tries to maximize the global utility function that takes into account the activities of all the agents in the system. Whereas, in local cooperation, two or more agents negotiating over an issue try to find a solution that increases the sum of their local utilities, without taking into account the rest of the agents in the system (Zhang et al. 2005). Various activities in the Semantic Web based systems such as seeking information from the Web sources, receiving tasks and preferences from the person, comparing information about user preferences etc. are performed by Semantic Web agents. The inter-agent dependencies among these agents are managed using the process of negotiation.

Following are some of the important topics related to automated negotiation:

Negotiation protocols are the set of rules governing the interaction process. It includes the permissible types of participants, negotiation states, the events causing negotiation states to change, and the valid actions of the participants in particular state (Jennings et al. 2001, Lomuscio et al. 2000).

Negotiation objects define the range of issues over which the agreement must be reached. It may contain a single issue such as price or multiple issues such as price, quality, time etc. The participants can have the flexibility to change the values of the issues in the negotiation object and even the participants might be allowed to dynamically alter the structure of negotiation object (Jennings et al. 2001; Lomuscio et al. 2000). The negotiation approach having multiple issues as the negotiation objects is called as multi-attribute negotiation. This type of negotiation process is widely used in the real-life scenario also.

Decision making models are employed by the participants to act in line with the negotiation protocol for achieving their objectives. The sophistication of the model is influenced by the negotiation protocol, nature of negotiation object, and by the range of operations that can be performed on it (Jennings et al. 2001, Lomuscio et al. 2000).

Negotiation strategy species the sequence of actions usually containing offers and responses that agent plans to make during the negotiation process. The choice of the negotiation strategy to use is a function of specifics of the negotiation scenario and the negotiation protocol to use. Thus, the strategies performing well with certain protocols may not do so with others (Lomuscio et al. 2000).

Negotiation mechanism consists of a negotiation protocol and negotiation strategies for the involved agents. A negotiation mechanism should have computational efficiency, communication efficiency, individual rationality, distribution of computation, and Pareto efficiency. The parameters based upon which negotiation can take place are categorized into many characteristics such as cardinality of negotiation, agent characteristics, environment and goods characteristics, event parameters, information parameters, and allocation parameters (Lomuscio et al. 2000).

References

G. Antoniou, Harmelen F.v, *A Semantic Web Primer* (The MIT Press, Cambridge 2004)

N.R. Jennings, P. Faratin, A.R. Lomuscio, S. Parsons, M.J. Wooldridge, C. Sierra, Automated negotiation: prospects, methods and challenges. Int. J. Gr. Decis. Negot. **10**(2), 199–215 (2001)

G. Kappel, B. Pröll, S. Reich, W. Retschitzegger, *Web Engineering* (Wiley, Hoboken, 2006)

A.R. Lomuscio, M. Wooldridge, N.R. Jennings, A Classification Scheme for Negotiation, in *Electronic Commerce. Agent-Mediated Electronic Commerce: A European Perspective*, ed. by F. Dignum, C. Sierra (Springer-Verlag, Berlin, 2000), pp. 19–33

H.J. Muller, *Negotiation Principles. John Wiley Sixth-Generation Computer Technology Series, Foundations of Distributed Artificial Intelligence Book* ed. by G.M.P. O'Hare, N.R. Jennings. (Wiley, New York, 1996), pp. 211–229

J. Rosenschein, G. Zlotkin, *Rules of Encounter: Designing Conventions for Automated Negotiation among Computers* (MIT Press, Cambridge, 1994)

K.P. Sycara, Multi-agent systems. AI Magazine, American Association for Artificial Intelligence **19**(2), 79–92 (1998)

M. Wooldridge, *An Introduction to multi-agent Systems* (Wiley, London, 2002)

X. Zhang, V. Lesser, R. Podorozhny, Multi-dimensional, multi-step negotiation for task allocation in a cooperative system. J. Auton. Ag. Multi-Ag. Syst. **10**(1), 5–40 (2005)

Chapter 3
Agent-Based Semantic Web Service Selection and Composition

Abstract The agent-based service composition system considers a service as an intelligent agent capability. In this system, a multi-agent system is considered as a Semantic Web Service composition system in which different agents represent the different individual services. The presented chapter discusses the basics of agent based service composition. An overview of some of the multi-agent based Semantic Web service composition approaches available in the literature has also been given. The chapter also presents models for agent-based Semantic Web service composition basically varying on the use of a coordinator agent in the composition process. Where, the coordinator agent is any agent that can control and coordinate all the different activities involved in the composition process. A brief overview of a service selection model providing formalization of various Quality of Service (QoS) parameters and cognitive parameters of agent for selecting the most appropriate service provider agent has also been presented.

Keywords Semantic Web · Multi-agent systems · Service selection · Service composition

3.1 Agent-Based Semantic Web Service Composition

Semantic Web Services (SWSs) can be obtained from web services by performing the augmentation of web service descriptions through Semantic Web annotations to facilitate the higher automation of service discovery, composition, invocation, and monitoring on the Web (Payne and Lassila 2004). SWSs can be developed by creating semantic mark-up of web services to make them computer-interpretable, user-apparent, and agent-ready. Semantic web service composition is considered to be the one of important process involved in satisfying the complex

S. Kumar, *Agent-Based Semantic Web Service Composition*,
SpringerBriefs in Electrical and Computer Engineering,
DOI: 10.1007/978-1-4614-4663-7_3, © The Author(s) 2012

client-requests. In most of the practical cases, the single web service is not able to satisfy the customer requirement because it is mostly the combination of multiple sub-requirements. In those cases, the process of SWS composition comes into play. The process of generating aggregated service by the integration of independent available component services for satisfying a client-request that cannot be satisfied by any single available service is called as SWS Composition. Whereas, a Multi-Agent System (MAS) consists of a team or organization of software agents collectively performing a task that could not be performed by any individual agent. Hence, the multiagent-based SWS composition is based upon the argument that a multi-agent system can be considered as a SWS composition system, in which different involved agents represent the different individual services. In this scenario, a service is considered as an intelligent agent capability implemented as a self-contained software component. Various agents in multi-agent system cooperate in a physically and possibly geographically distributed network to form a software system. Various agents participating in the multiagent system are able to communicate with each other. These are also capable of coordinating their activities (Ermolayev et al. 2004). There is a service requester agent (SRA) that needs services and sends request to other agent capable of providing services called as service provider agent (SPA). A lot of works on SWS composition are available such as (Gomez-Perez et al. 2004; Sell et al. 2004; Wu et al. 2003, 2006; Lecue and Leger 2006; Arpinar et al. 2004; Chen et al. 2003; Pistore et al. 2004; Vallee et al. 2005; Kungas and Matskin 2006; Agarwal et al. 2005; McIlraith and Son 2002; Kvaloy et al. 2005; Ermolayev et al. 2004; Charif and Sabouret 2005; and Kumar and Mishra 2008a). The works by (Kungas and Matskin 2006, 2005; Abela 2003; Ermolayev et al. 2004; Burstein et al. 2005; Vallee et al. 2005; Cao et al. 2005; Preist et al. 2001; Kungas et al. 2004; and Kumar and Mishra 2008a) are among the many works on agent-based SWS composition. Next section provides an overview of these works.

3.2 Overview of Some Works on Agent-Based SWS Composition

In this section, an overview of some of the works on agent-based SWS composition available in the literature is given. Among others, some of the reported works on SWS composition are (Preist et al. 2001; Abela 2003; Ermolayev et al. 2004; Kungas et al. 2004; Burstein et al. 2005; Vallee et al. 2005; Cao et al. 2005; Kungas and Matskin 2005, 2006; and Kumar and Mishra 2008a).

A multi-agent-based web service composition approach that can be used specifically for the composition of e-services has been presented (Preist et al. 2001). In this approach, multiple auctions are performed simultaneously with service requester as well as service providers. The approach generates the composite service dynamically.

Abela (2003) has presented an agent based composition engine. The different modules composing the engine are: Planner, Definer, Scheduler, Executer, Reasoning module, and Communication module. In the system, the Definer module generates the new DAML-S specifications from the individually composed service specifications. The communication module of the system uses Java Agent Development Framework (JADE) (JADE 2009) for communicating with user agents or other composition engines. The JTP (Java Theorem Prover) (Frank et al. 2008) has been used by the reasoning module for performing reasoning process. Various features of the presented composition engine providing automated composition includes: Use of DAML-S for service profile; performing scheduling of tasks; workflow planning; monitoring of execution process status; fault handling; communication with entities like agents and registries.

The work on multi-agent-based service composition presented by Ermolayev et al. (2004) is based upon the idea of using the agents' capabilities as service components. In this work, an agent based framework for service composition has been proposed that is capable of providing intelligent dynamic composition and hence can cop-up with the changes in environment affected by service execution flow. An agent-based middleware layer is used as a service mediator for scalable intelligent dynamic service composition. The incoming task is interpreted as task comprising of varying granularity and is decomposed on the basis of their local knowledge. The work has enlisted some of the following issues that might have been unsolved or were partially unsolved:

- No common mechanism for activity outsourcing.
- Unsufficient methodology for representation of tasks, activities, and services.
- Non-standardization of measurement, assesment, and evaluation of human-base parameters such as trust, credibility, reliability, and capability.

In this work, the service profiles are described using DAML-S. The various features of the composition process can be summarized as below:

- Perform composition by the dynamic coalition of service providing agents (SPAs) in the participating task.
- Decomposes the incoming task on the basis of their local knowledge/ontology.
- Perform selection of SPA for each of decomposed task.

Kungas et al. (2004) have proposed a composition approach based upon the symbolic agent negotiation that can be used as the mechanism for discovering available web services and composing them automatically. It involves the construction of a composite web service dynamically by initializing the symbolic agent negotiation between the agents. The architecture of the presented system is based upon the multi-agent system AGORA (Matskin et al. 2001). The service profiles are described using DAMS-S.

Burstein et al. (2005) have proposed a SWS composition approach based upon interactive agents. In this approach, the agents in SWSs are used as clients (requesters), service providers, and middle agents. The client specifies what they want from services. Three main functions related to composition of SWSs in this method are: service discovery, engagement, and enactment. Using service discovery, agent identifies required services to achieve its objective. Service engagement is applied to engage agents on agreements on some terms. Service enactment is applied to perform dynamic service composition finally.

In their work, (Vallee et al. 2005) have proposed an approach for combining multiagent techniques with SWSs to enable dynamic, context-aware service composition in ambient intelligence environments. Various benefits of using coupling of service-oriented approach and multiagent systems in ambient intelligence environment have been discussed. It is found that such environment is able to provide more appropriate interactions with users. But, the work has not discussed the architectural detail of the proposed approach and various processes involved.

Cao et al. (2005) have proposed a SWS composition approach in which the SWS composition problem has been modeled as a constraint satisfaction problem. The approach is based upon the multiagent negotiation and the multiagent negotiation algorithm has been applied for solving such obtained constraint satisfaction problem. The proposed approach deals with the end-user on-demand service requirements.

Kungas and Matskin (2005) have extended their earlier work (Kungas et al. 2004) on agent-based Semantic Web Service composition using combination of symbolic and non-symbolic negotiation. The symbolic negotiation has been used for dynamic web service discovery and composition. The non-symbolic negotiation has been used for negotiating over the cost or other such attributes of composite service.

A multi-agent system for service composition as well as service discovery of SWSs based on the chord P2P network (Stoica et al. 2001) has been presented by Kungas and Matskin (2006). The system provides a distributed composition of SWSs by applying agent technologies on structured P2P networks. The reasoning over the services is performed using domain ontologies during the partial deduction process. The system provides dynamic composition of services using agents, which cooperatively apply distributed symbolic reasoning. The Semantic Web Ontology Language, OWL-S, is used in the system for describing the services. The composition process mainly involves following steps:

- The available SWSs are taken as input from OWL-S service profiles.
- The input services are transformed into linear logic formulae.
- Partial deduction is applied on the linear logic formulae to get the requested solution.
- The final solution is transformed into the OWL-S service profile and returned to the requester.
- If the solution obtained is partial and not complete, it can be extended using a Cooperative Problem Solving Framework to get the complete solution.

Kumar and Mishra (2008a) have presented a multiagent-based SWS composition process based upon the understanding of using agent capability as an SWS component and using various cognitive parameters for service selection. A framework for intelligent dynamic service composition using the concept of independent coordinator agent to control the composition process has been presented. The work has also presented formal models for service selection. Two models for agent selection have been proposed. The models are based upon the formalization of various quality attributes of the service provider as well as formalization of cognitive parameters of the service provider such as trust, reputation, intention, capability, desire, commitment etc. The presented selection model has been used for formalization of both quality parameters and cognitive parameters that further generates an index of selection to be used for ranking of various discovered service providers.

3.3 Multi-Agent-Based Semantic Web Service Composition Model

Most of the work available on multiagent-based SWS composition is based upon the concept that a multi-agent system (MAS) can be considered as a SWS composition system in which different involved agents represent the different individual services. In these MASs, the participating agents are capable of coordinating their activities and to communicate with each other (Ermolayev et al. 2004). Multiagent-based SWS composition models depending on the variations in the composition process have been presented by author of this chapter (Kumar and Mishra 2008b). This section provides a detailed discussion on this work.

The presented models for SWS composition basically vary on the use of coordinator agent in the composition process. It is argued that there can be an agent that will be responsible for coordinating all the different activities involved in the composition process ranging from decomposition of the composite request into multiple atomic tasks to selection of various service provider agents for each of these tasks. This agent is called as coordinator agent. In this scenario, in addition to the coordination activities the coordinator agent may also be performing some of the atomic tasks out of total atomic tasks obtained from the decomposition of composite request. Depending upon this, there are following three possible types of SWS composition process (Kumar and Mishra 2008b):

Case 1: Composition process in which no coordinator agent is used (Fig. 3.1)

Case 2: Composition process in which a dedicated coordinator agent is there and it is only performing the activities involved in composition process (Fig. 3.2)

Case 3: Composition process that uses a coordinator agent which in addition to coordinating the composition process also performs some of the atomic tasks (Fig. 3.3)

The selection of most appropriate service provider agents capable of performing various atomic tasks can be performed using their quality of service and cognitive parameters. A brief overview of one of such model is presented in the next section. The composition models presented in Case 1 and Case 2 that are using coordinator are more advantageous than the other one. It is due to the reason

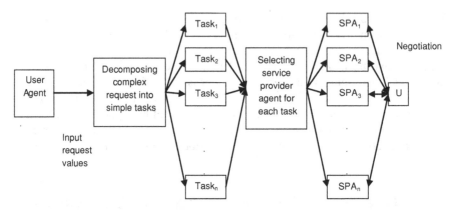

Fig. 3.1 Case 1 (Kumar and Mishra 2008b)

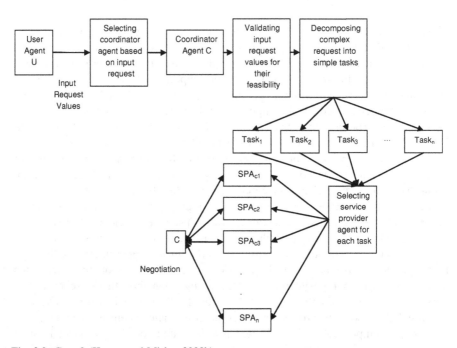

Fig. 3.2 Case 2 (Kumar and Mishra 2008b)

that in these models some of the constraints and parameters put by the user are validated by the coordinator agent before performing the actual composition process and hence saving the time and resources. Some of the constraints such as constraint over the budget, constraint over the time in which the complete request has to be satisfied and others are there which cannot be checked by any one of the SPAs, because these are not related to any one of the decomposed tasks but are related to the goal input-request. So, in these cases, the coordinator agent can be

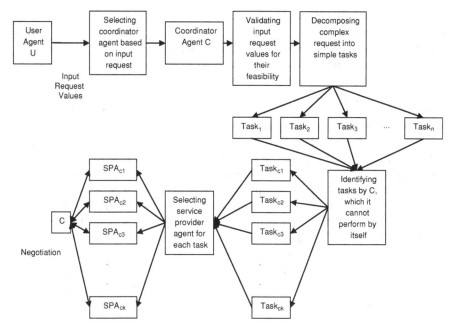

Fig. 3.3 Case 3 (Kumar and Mishra 2008b)

made to check whether the constraints seem to be satisfiable up-to a level or are clearly unsatisfiable. So in case of unsatisfiablity, coordinator can warn the service requester agent about it and there will be no need to move further in the composition process.

3.4 Quality of Service and Cognitive Parameters-Based Service Selection Model

The agent in MAS-based SWS composition systems can be characterized by various social, cognitive, and Quality of Service (QoS) parameters and hence a reliable selection of most appropriate SWSs can be achieved. A formal model providing selection of intelligent software agent based on its cognitive and QoS parameters for MAS-based SWS composition has been presented (Kumar and Mishra 2008c). Various cognitive parameters such as capability, desire, intention, commitment, trust, reputation etc. and a number of QoS parameters such as cost, response time, reliability, accuracy, security feature, execution time, exception handling feature, penalty on breaking service contract etc. have to be considered in service selection. The QoS can be defined as a part of service description and is an especially important factor for service composition (Zeng et al. 2004). The cognitive parameters of service providers can also prove to be the deciding factors in semantic web service selection and composition. The presented selection model performs rating of the agents based on their cognitive as well as QoS parameters. In the presented model, a formalization of various QoS parameters has been given. The work has also presented a novel normalization procedure for various QoS parameters. The formalization of various cognitive parameters and method for measuring the reputation of agent has also been proposed. The work has also presented a dynamic feedback system affecting the reputation of the selected service provider based on the quality of its present service.

The presented selection model (Kumar and Mishra 2008c) generates an Index of Selection (IoS) representing the overall rating of agent based on its cognitive parameters-based rating and QoS parameters-based rating as weighted sum of both. The QoS-based rating of an agent has been defined as the weighted arithmetic mean of the quality ratings of different QoS parameters after their normalization. The normalization of various quality metrics is required because they have different value ranges, value types, measurements and user tendency. Some of the quality metrics have user tendency of 'lower the better' and others have the 'higher the better'. A normalization of metrics has been provided such that value of all metrics lie between 0 and 1 and they all are of the tendency 'higher the better'. Hence, the quality based rating of agent is represented as below:

$$
QI = \frac{\sum_{i=1}^{t} Ql'_i * WQ_i \quad + \quad \sum_{i=(t+1)}^{n} Qh'_i * WQ_i}{\sum_{i=1}^{n} WQ_i}
$$

where,

- QI is the quality-based rating of agent and holds $\quad 0 < QI \le 1$
- $\{Ql_1, Ql_2 \ldots Ql_t, Qh_{t+1}, Qh_{t+2} \ldots Qh_n\}$ is the set of published numerical values for n quality attributes. Out of the n attributes, the first t attributes i.e. $(Ql_1, Ql_2 \ldots Ql_t)$, have the user tendency 'lower the better', while the next $(n - t)$ attributes i.e. $(Qh_{t+1}, Qh_{t+2} \ldots Qh_n)$, have the user tendency 'higher the better'.
- $WQ_1, WQ_2 \ldots WQ_n$ be the quality weights given to set of quality attributes.
- Ql'_k be the normalized value for quality attribute Ql_k, where $k = 1, 2 \ldots t$. It is represented by following relation:

$$
Ql'_k = 1 - \left(\frac{Ql_k - Ql\min_k}{Ql\max_k + Ql\min_k} \right)
$$

- Qh'_k be the normalized value for quality attribute Qh_k, where $k = (t + 1)$, $(t + 2) \ldots n$. It is represented by following relation:

$$Qh'_k = \frac{Qh_k}{Qh\max_k}$$

- $Ql\max_k$ and $Ql\min_k$ be the maximum and minimum numerical values for the attribute Ql_k among all the candidate profiles of agents.

The cognition parameters-based rating judges the trustworthiness and reputation of agent. So, it is defined as the weighted sum of trustworthiness and reputation of agent. For measuring the reputation of agent, the work has proposed an architecture in which each of the service requester agent maintains a separate Reputation Table in its service profile, which has reputation indexes of SPAs from its own point of view. The overall value for reputation of SPA will be the weighted arithmetic mean of the reputation indexes from all the SRAs including the given SRA itself. A formulation for measurement of reputation has been provided. Further, the work also provides the formulation for calculation of trust ultimately depending on the various parameters-based upon the past performance of the agents towards the tasks assigned to them. Based upon the work in (Barber and Kim 2001), the trust has been represented as the multiplication of capability and intention of agent. Further, based upon the arguments presented in (Tweedale et al. 2007; Cohen and Levesque 1990), the intention has been represented as the combination of desire and commitment. The formulation for the capability, desire and commitment has been provided based the past performance of concerned agent towards the various tasks assigned to it in past.

References

C. Abela, *Semantic Web Services Composition. Computer Science Annual Research Workshop* (Malta Council for Science and Technology, Kalkara, 2003)

S. Agarwal, S. Handschuh, S. Staab, Annotation, composition and invocation of semantic web services. J. Web Semant. **2**(1), 1–24 (2005)

I.B. Arpinar, B. Aleman-Meza, R. Zhang, A. Maduko, Ontology-Driven Web Services Composition Platform. In *Proceedings of IEEE International Conference on E- Commerce Technology, CEC'04* (IEEE Press, San Diego, 2004), pp. 146–152

K.S. Barber, J. Kim, Belief revision process based on trust: agents evaluating reputation of information sources. Lect. Notes Comput. Sci. **2246**, 73–82 (2001)

M. Burstein, C. Bussler, M. Zaremba, T. Finin, M. Huhns, M. Paolucci, A. Sheth, S. Williams, A semantic web services architecture. IEEE Internet Comput. **9**, 72–81 (2005)

J. Cao, J. Wang, S. Zhang, M. Li, A multi-agent negotiation based service composition method for on demand service. In proceedings of the 2005 IEEE international conference on services computing (SCC'05). IEEE Comput. Soc. **1**, 329–332 (2005)

Y. Charif, N. Sabouret, An overview of semantic web services composition approaches. Electron. Notes Theor. Comput. Sci. Elsevier Sci **85**(6), 1–8 (2005)

L. Chen, N.R. Shadbolt, C. Goble, F. Tao, S.J. Cox, C. Puleston, P.R. Smart, *Towards a Knowledge-based Approach to Semantic Service Composition*. Lecture Notes in Computer Science, vol. 2870 (Springer, Berlin, 2003), pp. 319–334

P.R. Cohen, H.J. Levesque, Intention is choice with commitment. Artif. Intell. Elsevier **42**(2–3), 213–261 (1990)

V. Ermolayev, N. Keberle, O. Kononenko, S. Plaksin, V. Terziyan, Towards a framework for agent-enabled semantic web service composition. Int. J. Web Serv. Res. **1**(3), 63–87 (2004)

G. Frank, J. Jenkins, R. Fikes, JTP: an object-oriented modular reasoning system (2008), http://ksl.stanford.edu/software/JTP/. Accessed 16 June 2009. 22 Jan 2008 (website last updated)

A. Gomez-Perez, R. Gonzalez-Cabero, M. Lama, Framework for Design and Composition of SWS based on Stack of Ontologies. In *Proceedings of Semantic Web Services 2004 AAAI Spring Symposium Series*, 22nd–24th March (2004)

JADE, Java Agent Development Framework (2009), http://jade.tilab.com/. Accessed 16 Feb 2009

S. Kumar, R.B. Mishra, A framework towards semantic web service composition based on multi-agent system. Int. J. Inf. Technol. Web Eng. IGI USA **3**(4), 59–81 (2008a)

S. Kumar, R.B. Mishra, Multi-agent based semantic web service composition models. J. Comput. Sci. Infocomp **7**(3), 42–51 (2008b)

S. Kumar, R.B. Mishra, A hybrid model for service selection in semantic web service composition. Int. J. Intell. Inf. Technol, IGI USA **4**(4), 55–69 (2008c)

P. Kungas, M. Matskin, Combining Symbolic and Non-Symbolic Negotiation for Agent-Based Web Service Composition. In *Proceedings of the 2005 International Conference on Artificial Intelligence ICAI'05* (CSREA Press, Las Vegas, 2005), pp. 513–519

P. Kungas, M. Matskin, Semantic Web Service Composition through a P2P-Based Multi-Agent Environment. In *Proceedings of the Fourth International Workshop on Agents and Peer-to-Peer Computing*, Netherlands, 2005. Lecture Notes in Computer Science, vol. 4118 (Springer-Verlag, Berlin, 2006), pp. 106–119

P. Kungas, J. Rao, M. Matskin, *Symbolic Agent Negotiation for Semantic web Service Exploitation* 2004. Lecture Notes in Computer Science, vol. 3129 (Springer, Berlin, 2004), pp. 458–467

T.A. Kvaloy, E. Rongen, A. Tirado-Ramos, P. Sloot, *Automatic Composition and Selection of Semantic Web Services* 2005. Lecture Notes in Computer Science, vol. 3470 (Springer-Verlag, Berlin, 2005), pp. 184–192

F. Lecue, A. Leger, A Formal Model for Semantic Web Service Composition. In *Proceedings of 5th International Semantic Web Conference*, Athens, 2006. Lecture Notes in Computer Science, vol. 4273 (Springer-Verlag, Heidelberg, 2006), pp. 385–398

M. Matskin, O.J. Kirkeluten, S.B. Krossnes, S. Sæle, A*gora: An Infrastructure For Cooperative Work Support In Multi-Agent Systems*, ed. by T. Wagner, O.F. Rana, International Workshop on Infrastructure for Multi-Agent Systems, Barcelona 2001. Lecture Notes in Computer Science, vol. 1887, (Springer-Verlag, Berlin, 2001), pp. 28–40

S. Mcllraith, T.C. Son, Adapting Golog for Composition of Semantic Web services. In *Proceedings of the Eighth International Conference on Knowledge Representation and Reasoning (KR2002)*, (Toulouse, 2002), www.cs.toronto.edu/ ~ sheila/publications/mci-son-kr02.pdf, pp. 482–493

T. Payne, O. Lassila, Semantic web services. IEEE Intell. Syst. **19**(4), 14–15 (2004)

M. Pistore, P. Bertoli, E. Cusenza, A. Marconi, P. Traverso, WS-GEN: A Tool for the Automated Composition of Semantic Web Services. *Proceedings of International Semantic Web Conference* (ISWC, 2004), (Hiroshima, 2004), November 9–11

C. Preist, A. Byde, C. Bartolini, G. Piccinelli, Towards agent-based service composition through negotiation in multiple auctions. AISB J. **1**(1) (2001). http://www.aisb.org.uk

D. Sell, F. Hakimpour, J. Domingue, E. Motta, R. Pacheco, Interactive Composition of WSMO-based Semantic Web Services in IRS-III. In *Proceedings of the AKT Workshop on Semantic Web Services (AKT-SWS04)*, (2004)

I. Stoica, R. Morris, D. Karger, M.F. Kaashoek, H. Balakrishnan, A. Chord, Scalable Peer-to-Peer Lookup Service for Internet Applications. In *Proceedings of ACM SIGCOMM* (ACM Press, San Diego, 2001), pp. 149–160

J. Tweedale, N. Ichalkaranje, C. Sioutis, B. Jarvis, A. Consoli, G. Phillips-Wren Innovations in multi-agent systems. J. Netw. Comput. Appl. Elsevier Sci. **30**(3), 1089–1115 (2007)

M. Vallee, F. Ramparany, L. Vercouter (2005) A Multi-Agent System for Dynamic Service Composition in Ambient Intelligence Environments. In *Proceedings of Third International Conference on Pervasive Computing, PERVASIVE.* pp. 175–182

D. Wu, B. Parsia, E. Sirin, J. Hendler, D. Nau, Automating DAML-S Web Services Composition Using SHOP2. In *Proceedings of the 2nd International Semantic Web Conference (ISWC 2003)* (Sanibel Island, 2003)

Z. Wu, A. Ranabahu, K. Gomadam, A.P. Sheth (2006) Miller automatic semantic web services composition, www.cs.uga.edu/~jam/papers/zLSDISpapers/zixin.doc. Accessed 16 June 2009

L.Z. Zeng, B. Benatallah, H.H.N. Anne, M. Dumas, J. Kalagnanam, H. Chang, QoS-aware middleware for web service composition. IEEE Trans. Softw. Eng. **30**(5), 311–327 (2004)

Chapter 4
Multi-Attribute Negotiation Between Semantic Web Agents

Abstract In the real-life scenario, there are very common situations involving negotiation based upon the multiple issues simultaneously. In the same way, the negotiation before selection of any web service provider agent is based upon the multiple attributes of web service. This process of making a joint decision by two or more parties resulting into a mutually acceptable agreement on some matter involving multiple attributes is called as multi-attribute negotiation. After a brief discussion over the multi-attribute negotiation, the chapter presents an overview of some of available multi-attribute negotiation approaches. An agent-based, utility-based, multi-attribute negotiation approach providing negotiation between Semantic Web Services has been described in detail. This approach also presents the formalized modeling for utility calculation and the process for generation of proposals at different steps of negotiation.

Keywords Semantic Web · Multi-agent systems · Negotiation · Web services · Multi-attribute negotiation

4.1 Multi-Attribute Negotiation

Negotiation is the process by which a group of agents come to a mutually acceptable agreement on some matter. It is the process of making a joint decision by two or more parties. Among others, the negotiation object is considered to be the one of most important topic in automatic negotiation research. Negotiation object defines the range of issues over which the agreement must be reached. The object may contain a single issue such as price or it may contain multiple issues such as price, timing, quality etc. The negotiation approach, the negotiation-object of which contains multiple issues, is called as multi-attribute negotiation (MAN) approach. Further, the values of various issues in negotiation-object may be fixed or flexible to change (Jennings et al. 2001). They may be called as non-negotiable or negotiable issues respectively. Multi-attribute negotiation is a useful mechanism in real life (Lai et al. 2006). There are common situations where people must negotiate multiple issues simultaneously. Multi-attribute negotiation involves the use of multiple attributes of SWSs for negotiation. The proposal between SPA (service provider agent) and SRA (service requester agent) contains the values for multiple attributes and decision of agreement is taken based upon their combined values. Some of the works proposing models for multi-attribute negotiation are (Stamoulis et al. 1999; Jonker et al. 2007; Zhang et al. Zhang et al. 2005; Makedon et al. 2003; Huang and Sycara 2002; Rebstock and Thun 2003; Xiaolong et al. 2006; Rebstock 2001; Fei and Chen 2007; Chen et al. 2002). In the multi-attribute negotiation approaches, the final agreed values of different involved attributes such as price, time, quality etc. are obtained after the successful negotiation. Some of the multi-attribute negotiation approaches are based on the utility theory and involves the calculation of a utility value. These approaches have two variations: calculation of combined utility of SRA and SPA and taking the decision of negotiation on the attribute-values maximizing the combined utility; or calculation of individual utilities of SRA and SPA and getting the agreement of negotiation on the attributes-values on which the values of utilities of both SRA and SPA obtained an acceptable limit. The utility of a SRA/SPA represents its happiness or preference. Some of the works based on utility-based negotiation are (Stamoulis et al. 1999; Jonker et al. 2007; Zhang et al. 2005; Makedon et al. 2003; Xiaolong et al. 2006). The finally agreed values of various attributes involved in the negotiation-process and the achieved utility value after the successful negotiation can be used for the selection of SWSs. A model for the same purpose has been presented in the Chap. 5.

4.2 Overview of Some Multi-Attribute Negotiation Approaches

In this section, some of the multi-attribute negotiation approaches reported in the literature have been summarized.

A utility-based multi-attribute negotiation approach for multi-agent systems has been proposed by Jonker et al. (2007). They have presented the concept of financial utility and ease utility in the negotiation process.

The work by Zhang et al. (2005) has presented the multi-dimensional, multi-step, multi-attribute negotiation from multi-agent perspectives only. They have presented the utility-calculation for cooperative negotiation between agents. Though, their utility-calculation also does not consider the interdependence of different attributes. In this work, the concept of negotiation cost has been discussed in enough detail. The description of opportunity cost and opportunity gain has been given without discussion of their formal computation.

Makedon et al. (2003) have presented a Secure Content Exchange Negotiation System (SCENS) for multi-agent systems. It consists of three layers. First layer for web-based negotiation support system, second layer providing negotiation web services to end-user, and third layer providing open and automated negotiation environment. The work provides a good amount of discussion on the first two layers. Also, they have proposed a formal modeling of utility function, but their utility function is just a simple weighted sum of the values of various attributes without considering other involved factors.

A multi-attribute negotiation framework based on multi-agent systems for large-scale construction projects supply chain coordination has been proposed by Xiaolong et al. (2006). In this work, the supply chain has been considered as a typical multi-agent system. They have represented the target utility, TU, as: $TU = U_{BOW} + CS$, where U_{BOW} is the utility of own decision-making and CS is concession step. CS is determined by: $CS = \beta(1 - \mu/U_{BOW})(U_{BOT} - U_{BOW})$, where U_{BOT} is the utility of other participant's decision-making, μ is the minimal utility, and β is the negotiation speed. However, it has been seen that the model for utility determination presented by them represents the target utility in the form of other type of utility values. Their model can be helpful in the utility determination, but does not seem to provide concrete results for the target utility. No discussion has been found on the computation of U_{BOT} and U_{BOW}.

Stamoulis et al. (1999) have presented a multi-attribute negotiation approach and a utility model especially suited to the telecommunication domain. They have represented the total utility of a service combination, S, by following equation: $u(S) = \sum_c k_c u_c$, where k_c is the weight of a content-section and u_c is the utility associated with a content-section. Further, the u_c has been computed as the weighted sum of the utilities of constituent medias, $u_m(q_m)$, by following equation: $u_c = \sum_{m \in M_c} \rho_m^c u_m(q_m)$, where ρ_m^c is the weight of medium m. However, no discussion has been found on the computation of $u_m(q_m)$.

A multi-attribute negotiation model with incomplete information has been proposed by Lai et al. (2006). They have also presented a time-dependent negotiation strategy. In this strategy, a formulation for the utility that an agent desires to get in a time-period has been presented. However, they have represented the utility in the form of other utility-values. They have proposed the following relation:

$$s_i(t) = 1 - (1 - ru_i)\left(\frac{t}{T_i}\right)^{\frac{1}{\beta_i}}$$

where, $s_i(t)$ is the utility that agent N_i desires to get in the current period t, 1 is the maximal utility agent N_i can get from the negotiation, ru_i represents the ultimate reservation utility of agent N_i for this negotiation, T_i is the deadline of agent N_i, and β_i represents the strategy parameter of agent N_i. It can be easily observed from this relation that the utility $s_i(t)$ has been represented in the form of other utility value ru_i. But, no formulation has been found corresponding to ru_i.

Lai and Sycara (2009) have presented an automated multi-attribute negotiation framework. As part of the negotiation strategy of an agent, they have presented two mechanisms. First one is shortest-distance proposing mechanism and second is Pareto optimal mediating mechanism. These mechanisms are used for generating the proposal to be offered to the opponent agent. However, the negotiation strategy presented by them uses the same utility function as presented in the Lai et al. (2006) and hence have same drawback as depicted for the utility function of Lai et al. (2006).

Paurobally et al. (2005) presents the negotiation protocol and strategies for SWSs by refining and adapting the work on multi-agent systems particularly Rubinstein's alternating offers protocol (Rubinstein 1982).

Olmedilla et al. (2004) has presented a trust negotiation approach between semantic web services. They have used peer-trust languages for deciding that the trust can be established between SRA and SPA or not. They have discussed the use of different service-matchmakers. However, in this work, very little discussion over the negotiation environment and the formalized modeling of negotiation process could be found.

Nejdl et al. (2004) deals with the trust negotiation between peers over the Semantic Web. They have presented various issues involved in the trust negotiation and have proposed the method of representing appropriate policies and negotiation rules using distributed logic programs. However, very little discussion over the negotiation process has been found.

A utility-based multi-attribute negotiation approach for Semantic Web Services has been proposed by author of this book in (Kumar and Mishra 2009). The proposed negotiation approach mainly focuses on the computation of utility-factor, communication model, and an extension of traditional negotiation approach by using concepts of opportunity-cost, opportunity-gain, and negotiation-effort. It presents a utility-based multi-attribute negotiation for Semantic Web Services (SWSs). The next section discusses this approach in more detail. The presented negotiation approach tries to fulfill some of the shortcomings enumerated in the approaches discussed above.

4.3 A Multi-Attribute Negotiation Approach

A utility-based, multi-attribute negotiation model for negotiation between SWSs has been presented (Kumar and Mishra 2009). It has presented a communication model for the negotiation between SRA and SPA using FIPA Communicative Acts (FIPA TC C 2002). The step-by-step description of the negotiation process along with the algorithms for various activities has also been presented.

A utility model has been proposed, which is based on a novel understanding that if the price, response-time, or other such factors are changed appropriately according to the change in quality, then the utility should remain intact. The proposed utility model considers multiple attributes such as price, quality, and response-time in utility-calculation and is easily adaptable to also consider other such attributes, if required. This work also provides the extension of the utility model by proposing the use of other important factors in the decision-making such as opportunity-cost, opportunity-gain and negotiation-effort. In addition, the work also presents the formalization of these parameters to provide their accurate calculation. The utility model presents the formalization of various parameters in the form of values of basic attributes such as price, quality etc., which are easily available during the negotiation process. These factors make this approach more in line with the practical manual negotiation process. Further, the presented negotiation model has proposed a feedback-system by presenting a new data-structure, The Agreement-Table. It stores the results of successful negotiations with a SRA that can be used in handling the negotiation-request from the same SRA in future. This will expedite the negotiation process by reaching the agreement in lesser number of negotiation-steps. The work also presents the implementation of a prototype system providing negotiation based on the proposed approach along with the service description profiles of SPAs and SRA in ontological form using OWL (McGuinness and Harmelen 2004). Hence, this negotiation approach for SWSs seems to be more reliable, can provide more accurate decision-making, can fasten the process, and is more in line with the practical manual negotiation process.

The multi-attribute negotiation environment described in this work (Kumar and Mishra 2009) contains a set of SPAs (service provider agents) that offer computer-based services to their clients i.e. SRAs (service requester agents), which themselves may be service providers. Each SPA is an independent entity with attached service profile and is motivated by some business concerns such as achieving profitability and hence demands some payment for providing services. This approach also presents a feedback-system, which on successful negotiation stores the agreement into the Agreement-Table (AT). AT is a data-structure maintained by the SPA in its service profile and holds the values of various attributes of the latest agreement with a SRA that agreed to use its services. AT for a service provider agent contains agreement values for the recent agreement between a service requester agent and the service provider agent and an identifier representing the corresponding service requester agent. These values can help in the future negotiations between the SRA and the corresponding SPA to reach the agreement in less number of negotiation steps and hence saving time and efforts.

This approach involves the use of multiple attributes of SWSs for negotiation. The proposal between SPA and SRA contains the values for multiple attributes and decision of agreement is taken based upon their combined value. A utility value is used that is dependent on the values of all the attributes and represents the preference of corresponding SWS. The initial values of various attributes and conditions for termination of negotiation between SWSs can be fetched from their corresponding service profiles. During negotiation, the communication between SRA and SPA has been performed based upon the cooperative negotiation using

Communicative Acts of FIPA (FIPA TC C 2002). The negotiation process involves the generation of new proposals by both SRA and SPA and to check the proposal for termination of negotiation process. The process is terminated when either the agreement is reached or the number of negotiation steps reaches to a threshold value. The agreement between the SPA and SRA is reached when their corresponding utility-value reaches up to an acceptable value. A lot of work on the utility calculation (Jonker et al. 2007; Zhang et al. 2005; Makedon et al. 2003; Xiaolong et al. 2006; Stamoulis et al. 1999; Lai et al. 2006) is available in the literature as listed in Sect. 4.2. However, a more efficient utility-calculation is provided in this work.

The presented utility calculation model has used the understanding described in (Wilkes 2008). It depicts that the SRA and SPA should be indifferent to the various combinations of values of the different attributes in proposal which produces same utility. So, utility function should be designed such that it produces same utility-value for this type of combinations. For a proposal with attributes (price, quality), if the quality is improved then the corresponding price can also be increased in the appropriate ratio. So, if the price has been increased in the required ratio only, then the utility should remain the same. The presented utility function is based upon same understanding. The presented model describes utility as the function of some service attributes such as price, quality and response-time. These attributes are further shown to be related to each other in following form:

$$price = f(quality)$$

$$price = f\left(\frac{1}{response - time}\right)$$

$$response - time = f(quality)$$

The work has firstly presented a formalized model for calculating the new price after considering the following parameters:

(i) Effect of change in quality on price
(ii) Effect of change in quality on response-time
(iii) Effect of change in response-time caused by quality-change on price. It is further mentioned that if the response-time is appropriately changed with quality as per (ii), then the effect mentioned at (iii) will be nil.

After the new price has been obtained, it is further used to calculate the utility of SRA and SPA.

The new price after considering the various parameters mentioned above is formulated as below:

$$P_{new} = P_{initial} + \left(\frac{\left(P_{initial} * \frac{K_{PQ}}{100} \left(\frac{Q_{new} - Q_{initial}}{Q_{initial}} * 100 \right) \right)}{100} \right)$$

$$+ \left(\frac{\left(P_{initial} * \frac{K_{PT}}{100} \left(\frac{T_{new} - T_{ANew}}{T_{new}} * 100 \right) \right)}{100} \right)$$

where, $P_{initial}$, $Q_{initial}$, $T_{initial}$ be the price, quality, and response-time of a service. Q_{new} is the new quality required.

K_{PQ} is the constant holding relation, $0 \le K_{PQ} \le 100$. Its value is decided by the service provider. It represents the percentage of the percentage-change in quality with which the price should be changed.

T_{new} is the new response time that should be after considering the effect of change in quality.

T_{ANew} is actual new response-time.

K_{PT} is the constant holding relation, $0 \le K_{PQ} \le 100$. Its value is decided by the service provider. It represents the percentage of the percentage-change in response-time from T_{new} to T_{ANew} with which the price should be changed. T_{new} is further represented as below:

$$T_{new} = T_{initial} + \left(\frac{\left(T_{initial} * \frac{K_{TQ}}{100} \left(\frac{Q_{new} - Q_{initial}}{Q_{initial}} * 100 \right) \right)}{100} \right)$$

where, K_{TQ} represents the percentage of the percentage-change in quality (ΔQ) with which the response-time should be changed and holds relation, $0 \le K_{PQ} \le 100$.

These relations are further used for the calculation of utilities of SRA and SPA. Consider $\langle P_{offer}, Q_{offer}, T_{offer} \rangle$ is the proposal obtained by SRA from SPA and $\langle P_{initial}, Q_{initial}, T_{initial} \rangle$ are the values on which SRA agrees. So, in this case, Q_{offer} can be treated as the new quality Q_{new}, and offered response-time T_{offer} as the actual response-time T_{ANew}. Then, using above relations, the value for required price P_{new} can be calculated, which is the value of price considered appropriate by the SRA for the offered quality and response-time. This value of price, P_{new}, which has been calculated by considering the effect of both quality-change and alternation in response-time, will represent the level at which SRA is happy for the offered quality and response-time. Whereas, P_{offer} is the price offered for given quality and response-time. So, the ratio of P_{new} and P_{offer} will represent the happiness/preference level of SRA. So, utility of SRA will be $Utility_{SRA} = \frac{P_{new}}{P_{offer}}$. From this relation, it can be seen that if the offered-price is more than the required-price, then the utility of SRA will be less than one and the proposal will not be accepted. In the similar fashion, the utility of SPA can be calculated. The only difference is that in the case of SPA, for the proposal to be acceptable, the offered price should be more than or equal to the required-price. Hence, the utility of SPA can be represented as: $Utility_{SPA} = \frac{P_{offer}}{P_{new}}$.

Further, the work (Kumar and Mishra 2009) has also presented the formalization of various parameters such as opportunity-cost, opportunity-gain, and negotiation-cost (Zhang et al. 2005) that can be used to provide more efficient utility model. On considering the opportunity-cost, opportunity-gain, and negotiation-effort, the value of utility for SRA and SPA has been represented as follows:

$Net\ Utility\ for\ SPA = Utility_{SPA} - Negotiation\text{-}Effort - Opportunity\text{-}Cost$

$Net\ Utility\ for\ SRA = Utility_{SRA} - Negotiation\text{-}Effort + Opportunity\text{-}Gain$

where,

Opportunity-Cost is the loss occurring to the SPA on committing a negotiation. When the SPA makes a commitment to perform a task, it loses the opportunity to perform another incoming task of possibly higher utility. A formulation for calculating this has also been presented.

Opportunity-Gain is the gain occurring to the SRA on importing the task to SPA. When SRA imports task, it leaves itself more freedom to accept another task of possibly higher utility. A formulation for calculating this has also been presented.

Negotiation-Effort represents the consumption of resources such as time, computational capability, communication capacity etc. during the negotiation process. Otherwise, these resources could be used for some other tasks. A formulation for calculating this has also been presented.

References

J. Chen, R. Anane, K. Chao, N. Godwin, Architecture of an Agent-based Negotiation Mechanism. *Proceedings of the 22nd International Conference on Distributed Computing Systems Workshops, IEEE* (2002)

Y. Fei, W. Chen, A Multi-agent, Multi-object and Multi-attribute Intelligent Negotiation Model. *Fourth International Conference on Fuzzy Systems and Knowledge Discovery* (FSKD 2007)

FIPA TC C (2002) FIPA Communicative act library specification, http://www.fipa.org/specs/fipa00037/. Accessed 01 March 2009. 06 Dec 2002 (website last updated)

P. Huang, K. Sycara, A computational model for online agent negotiation. Proceedings of the 35th Hawaii international conference on system sciences 2002, IEEE Comput. Soc. (2002)

N.R. Jennings, P. Faratin, A.R. Lomuscio, S. Parsons, M.J. Wooldridge, C. Sierra, Automated negotiation: prospects, methods and challenges. Int. J. Group Dec. Negot. 10(2), 199–215 (2001)

C.M. Jonker, V. Robu, J. Treur, An agent architecture for multi-attribute negotiation using incomplete preference information. J. Auton. Ag. Multi-Ag. Syst. 15(2), 221–252 (2007)

S. Kumar, R.B. Mishra, An approach to multi-attribute negotiation between semantic web services. Int. J. Web Eng. Technol. 5(2), 162–186 (2009)

G. Lai, K. Sycara, A generic framework for automated multi-attribute negotiation. Group Dec. Negot. J. 18, 169–187 (2009)

G. Lai, C. Li, K. Sycara, Efficient multi-attribute negotiation with incomplete information. Group Dec. Negot. J. 15, 511–528 (2006)

F. Makedon, S. Ye, Y. Zhao, On the Design and Implementation of a Web-based Negotiation System. 9th Panhellenic Conference in Informatics (PCI2003), (Thessaloniki, 2003)

D.L. McGuinness, F.V. Harmelen, OWL web ontology language overview (2004). W3C Recommendations 2004, W3C Website, http://www.w3.org/TR/owl-features/. Accessed 13 Feb 2008

W. Nejdl, D. Olmedilla, M. Winslett, PeerTrust: automated trust negotiation for peers on the semantic web. In proceedings of the workshop on secure data management in a connected world (SDM '04) in conjunction with 30th international conference on very large databases. Lect. Notes Comput. Sci. **3178**, 118–132 (2004)

D. Olmedilla, R. Lara, A. Polleres, H. Lausen, Trust Negotiation for Semantic Web Services. In *Proceedings of the 1st International Workshop on Semantic Web Services and Web Process Composition* (San Diego, 2004), pp. 81–95

S. Paurobally, V. Tamma, M. Wooldridge, *Cooperation and Agreement between Semantic Web Services*. W3C Workshop on Frameworks for Semantics in Web Services (Innsbruck, 2005)

M. Rebstock, Efficiency and Flexibility of Multi-Attribute Negotiations—The Role of Business Object Frameworks. *Proceedings of International Workshop on Database and Expert Systems Applications* (IEEE, 2001), pp. 742–746

M. Rebstock, P. Thun, Interactive multi-attribute electronic negotiations in the supply chain: design issues and an application prototype. Proceedings of the 36th Hawaii international conference on system sciences (HICSS'03), IEEE Comput. Soc. (2003)

A. Rubinstein, Perfect equilibrium in a bargaining model. Econometrica **50**(1), 97–109 (1982)

G.D. Stamoulis, D. Kalopsikakis, A. Kyrikoglou, C. Courcoubetis, Efficient agent-based negotiation for telecommunications services. Proceedings of global telecommunications conference (GLOBECOM '99). IEEE **3**, 1989–1996 (1999)

J. Wilkes, Utility functions, prices, and negotiation (2008). Technical report, HP laboratories, HPL-2008-81, www.hpl.hp.com/techreports/2008/HPL-2008-81.pdf. Accessed 16 June 2009

X. Xiaolong, W. Yaowu, S. Qiping, Agent based Multi-attribute Negotiation for Large-Scale Construction Project Supply Chain Coordination. *Proceedings of the 2006 IEEE/WIC/ACM International Conference on Web Intelligence and Intelligent Agent Technology (WI-IAT 2006 Workshops) (WI-IATW'06)*, IEEE Computer Society, IEEE, (2006)

X. Zhang, V. Lesser, R. Podorozhny, Multi-dimensional, multi-step negotiation for task allocation in a cooperative system. J. Auton. Ag. Multi-Ag. Syst. **10**(1), 5–40 (2005)

Chapter 5
A Multi-Agent Negotiation-Based Approach to Selection and Composition of Semantic Web Services

Sandeep Kumar and R. B. Mishra

Abstract In the semantic web service composition process, the evaluation of negotiation-agreements resulting from the negotiation between the service requester and various service providers can be used for the selection of best service provider. The chapter presents a semantic web service composition model for the same purpose. A mathematical model providing multi-attribute negotiation-based service selection using evaluation of negotiation-agreements has also been proposed. A prototype system has been implemented based upon the proposed service selection and composition models.

Keywords Semantic Web · Service composition · Negotiation · Agreements · Service selection

5.1 Introduction

Semantic Web Service (SWS) composition is the process of generating the aggregated service by the integration of independent available component services for satisfying a client-request that can not be satisfied by any single available service. Service selection is one of the most important parts of SWS composition process. It involves the selection of the most appropriate SWS for performing a particular task from the available similar services.

In agent-based SWS composition environment, the negotiation is performed between the service requester agent (SRA) and the selected service provider agent

Sandeep Kumar—Department of Electronics and Computer Engineering, Indian Institute of Technology Roorkee, Rookee 247667, India
R. B. Mishra—Department of Computer Engineering, Indian Institute of Technology (Banaras Hindu University), Varanasi, India

S. Kumar, *Agent-Based Semantic Web Service Composition*,
SpringerBriefs in Electrical and Computer Engineering,
DOI: 10.1007/978-1-4614-4663-7_5, © The Author(s) 2012

(SPA) usually. Using this process, both of these agents reach to a mutually acceptable agreement on some parameters such a quality, price etc. If negotiation is performed with all the available SPAs for a task, then each successful negoti-ation will result into a negotiation-agreement acceptable to the reference service requester as well as to the corresponding service provider. The selection can be applied on these negotiation-agreements to select the best one and the corre-sponding service provider can be selected as the reference service provider agent. This will result into more reliable and favorable selection as the selection has been performed for the best from among the all acceptable and most favorable agree-ments. The presented work is based upon the same understanding. The chapter presents a SWS composition approach based upon the negotiation-agreements. It mainly involves the selection of a coordinator agent and various SPAs. The coordinator agent controls various service composition activities. The selection of coordinator agent is performed using a cognition-based service selection model (Kumar and Mishra 2008b). A negotiation-agreement based service selection model has also been proposed for the selection of various SPAs. Based upon the proposed selection and composition models, a prototype service composition system has also been implemented. The evaluation and comparative analysis of proposed models have been performed and some related works have been pre-sented. Following is the main contribution of chapter:

- An approach for the composition of SWSs based upon their negotiation-agreements has been proposed.
- A service selection model has been proposed which presents the mathematical formulation for the selection of most appropriate SPA, based upon the negoti-ation-agreements of candidate SPAs.
- A prototype system has been implemented in support of the proposed models and its application to a domain area of education planning has been discussed.

The remainder of chapter is structured as follows. Section 5.2 discusses various reported works similar to our presented work. The model for the composition of semantic web services based upon negotiation-agreements has been presented in the Sect. 5.3. Section 5.4 deals with the model for selection of semantic web services based upon negotiation-agreements. The work has been evaluated in the Sect. 5.5. Section 5.6 presents the implementation of a prototype service com-position system.

5.2 Related Works

Some of the reported works similar to our proposed SWS selection and compo-sition approach are discussed in this section. Out of the many reported SWS selection and composition approaches, only few are there which provide negoti-ation-based selection and composition of SWSs. Some of them are (Cao et al. 2005; Kungas et al. 2004; Kungas and Matskin 2005; Preist et al. 2002). Cao et al.

2005 in their work on service composition have proposed a multi-agent negotiation-based service composition approach. The approach deals with the end-user on-demand service requirements. They have proposed a methodology for modeling the service composition as a constraint satisfaction problem and have used the multi-agent negotiation algorithm for solving it. Symbolic agent negotiation has been used as the mechanism for discovering available web services and composing them automatically by Kungas et al. 2004. In their mechanism, if no service satisfying user's requirements are found then the symbolic negotiation is initiated between the agents and the new composite web service is constructed dynamically. Their system architecture is based upon the multi-agent system AGORA (Matskin et al. 2001). Kungas and Matskin 2005 have extended the work of Kungas et al. 2004 to use the combination of symbolic and non-symbolic negotiation for agent-based web service composition. Apart from using the symbolic negotiation for dynamic web service discovery and composition, they have used the non-symbolic negotiation for negotiating over the cost or other such attributes of composite service. Preist et al. 2002 have proposed an agent-based web service composition approach for composition of e-services through negotiation in multiple simultaneous auctions. They have presented a practical example to show how the negotiation phase in service composition process can be used to perform the multiple auctions simultaneously with the customer as well as with the service providers and dynamically generating the composite service.

Similar to these reported works, our presented work also proposes a negotiation-based SWS selection and composition approach. These works have used the negotiation as a supporting process in service composition. In contrary to these, our work firstly performs the negotiation with all available SPAs and the result of negotiation is further used in the process of service selection. The presented work has proposed a service composition model providing such type of composition facility. Work has also presented a service selection model based upon the negotiation-agreements. A prototype system has also been implemented based upon the proposed models.

5.3 Negotiation-Agreement Based Composition Model

In this section, we have presented a novel model, Negotiation-Agreement based Composition Model (NACM), for the composition of SWSs. NACM is based upon the concept of performing the negotiation with all the eligible SPAs and selecting the final service provider from the SPAs with successful negotiation using their negotiation-agreements. NACM also uses an independent dedicated coordinator agent for controlling the various activities in composition process. A layout for NACM is shown in the Fig. 5.1(a) and (b). In NACM, mainly three types of SWS agents are used: service requester agent (SRA), service provider agent (SPA), and coordinator agent (CA).

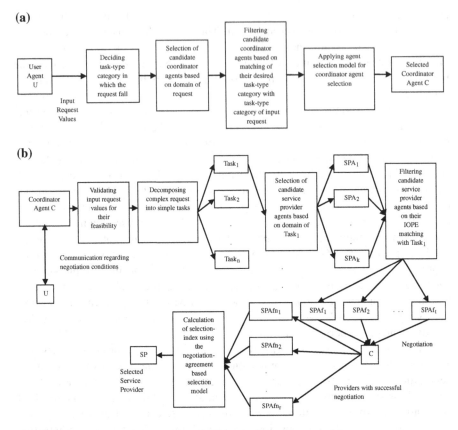

Fig. 5.1 a Coordinator agent selection, **b** SPA selection and composition

SRA has the responsibility to perform the request to CA. The request by SRA is then specified in the term of ontology, which is then used by the CA. CA is a modular, self-contained software component, wrapping coordination services, with ontological service description. It has the capability of validating the constraints, preferences, and other higher level parameters of the SRA's input-request. It has the capability of validating if the input activity is atomic or complex. In case it is complex, interpreting it as task comprising of various atomic activities of varying granularity and decomposing it into atomic tasks according to their ontology description. CA can negotiate with the SPAs using some negotiation approach, resulting into some common agreement over the various service-attributes. Further, it can evaluate and assess the SPAs based upon the nature of their negotiation-agreements. CA is also responsible for making the arrangement for outsourcing the activity to SPAs based on FIPA Contract Net Protocol (Smith and Davis 2008) and agent's communication interface built upon FIPA-ACL (FIPA Architecture Board 2008). SPA is a self-contained, modular agent, wrapping services in the form of software components, with the corresponding ontological service description. The purpose of SPA is decided by the services it wraps. It is able to understand the meaning of activity, it is to perform. SPA joins the composition process, only for the time its service is required.

Layouts of NACM are shown in Fig. 5.1(a) and (b), for CA and SPA selection respectively. NACM involves sending a request from the SRA, user agent U, to the system, which is then represented in the term of ontologies. The parameters in the request are used to decide the domain and further the task-type category within the domain of the request. The domain of the request is used to discover the candidate CAs by matching from their published ontological service profiles. The candidate CAs are further filtered based on the matching that if the task-type category of the input-request is matching with any of the category mentioned in the set of desired task-type categories of the candidate CA or not. The match-making here can be performed either using semantic matching (Paolucci et al. 2002) based on ontology profiles like in DAML-S (The DAML Services Coalition 2008), OWL (McGuinness and Harmelen 2008) or using any other service matching method. Various techniques of discovery (Stollberg and Haller 2005) can be applied here like keyword matching, controlled vocabulary matching, semantic matchmaking etc. The system can be made to proceed with the exact match, plug-in match, subsumption match, or intersection match as required in the process. Index of Selection (IoS) is then calculated for each of the filtered CAs using CPBSM (Kumar and Mishra 2008b) and the CA with maximum IoS is selected as the coordinator C for given composition problem. At this stage, U can perform negotiation with C-based on FIPA Contract Net Protocol (Smith and Davis 2008). The details on this process of selection of CA can be referred from (Kumar and Mishra 2008a).

C accepts task from U by means of agent's communication interface built upon FIPA-ACL (FIPA Architecture Board 2008). All further activities remaining in the NACM are coordinated by C. C performs a validation over the parameters, preferences, and constraints to check their feasibility. Request from SRA may contain such parameters, constraints, or preferences which seem infeasible or within specified constraints the satisfaction of request seems near to impossible. So, the composition will fail at the end, when even after negotiation between SPAs and CA, the constraints will not be satisfied. So, this validation at this point prevents this situation to occur. Further, it determines from the input-request that it is an atomic activity or complex one. In case the input request is complex task, then C decomposes it into atomic tasks, $Task_1$, $Task_2$ ... $Task_n$, of varying granularity. Now, for each atomic task, the candidate SPAs are discovered by using the same process as depicted above for discovery of CA. Consider that for the task $Task_1$, k numbers of SPAs are discovered i.e. SPA_1, SPA_2 ... SPA_k. Filtering over discovered SPAs is performed based on their IOPE (Inputs, Outputs, Pre-conditions, Effects) matching with the required task. The matchmaking at this stage can be performed in the similar way as described above for the CA. During this match-making process, some of the discovered SPAs get filtered and out of k numbers of discovered SPAs for $Task_1$, the t numbers of filtered SPAs are $SPAf_1$, $SPAf_2$ ... $SPAf_t$. Now, C performs negotiation with each of the filtered SPAs using any of negotiation approach. The negotiation approach here can be a multi-attribute negotiation approach or a utility-theory based negotiation approach or other similar. The approach should be such that after successful negotiation it generates an agreement composed of the finally agreed values of various service-attributes such as price, quality, response-time etc. at which both C and SPA agrees. It may be the possibility that during the negotiation with some of the SPAs, up to a threshold-limit of negotiation, no mutual agreement takes place. For $Task_1$, out of the t numbers of filtered agents, the r numbers of agents with successful negotiation are $SPAfn_1$, $SPAfn_2$ ... $SPAfn_r$. Now, for each of these SPAs, the proposed NASM (Negotiation-Agreement based Selection Model) is applied to calculate an index of selection and the SPA with maximum index is selected as the provider agent for performing the corresponding task. NASM is a mathematical model for the selection of most appropriate SPA, based upon the negotiation-agreements of candidate SPAs. Using the negotiation-agreements of candidate SPAs, NASM calculates an index of selection and the agent with maximum index is selected. For each of the decomposed tasks, the same process is followed for the selection of corresponding SPA. After SPAs for all the tasks have been selected, interfacing and communication is established between them to aggregate them into a composite service. NASM has been presented in detail in the forthcoming section.

5.4 Negotiation-Agreement Based Selection Model

Based upon the concepts described in the Chap. 3 on multi-attribute negotiation, two methods for selection of SPA are possible:

(1) Using the values of utility-factors of various candidate SPAs.
(2) Using the values of various attributes after the successful negotiation with candidate SPAs.

In the first method, firstly the utility-theory based negotiation is performed with the various candidate SPAs. This results into the values of utility-factor for those candidate SPAs, with which the negotiation results into successful agreement. The value of this utility factor represents the happiness or preference of SRA for the corresponding SPA. So, the SPA with which the utility-factor is highest is the service provider to which SRA is providing highest preference or is most happy with. So, the SPA with highest utility-factor can be selected as the final SWS provider. But, there are following drawbacks of this approach:

(a) In this method, the weightage of different attributes in SPA selection is the same as in utility-calculation. If one want to give different weights, then it is not possible.
(b) This method is applicable only if the negotiation between the SRA and SPAs has been performed using the utility-based negotiation approach.

In the second selection method, firstly the negotiation is performed with the various candidate SPAs using any selected negotiation approach. Independent of the approach used for negotiation, it will result into some agreed-values of various involved attributes if the negotiation is successful. Using these values of various attributes, an index of selection (IoS) is calculated using the model described below and the SPA with highest IoS is selected. During the calculation of IoS, the desired weights can be given to the various attributes. Thus, both of the drawbacks depicted for the first method get resolved. The calculation of IoS for a SPA is shown below.

5.4.1 Calculation of Index of Selection

After the successful negotiation of a SRA with a SPA, a set of values of various involved attributes is resulted at which both SRA and SPA agree. This set of values of various attributes can be called as agreement-set of SRA with respect to SPA. A SRA, before performing the negotiation, usually has some expectations about the values of various attributes of the service. This set of values of various attributes can be called as expectation-set of SRA. Now, from a successful negotiation of a SRA with a SPA, a SRA must have some overall gain from its agreement-set with respect to its expectation-set. However, for some of the parameters in the set, it may be losing and for some others it may be gaining. The gain of a SRA with respect to a SPA directly depends upon their corresponding agreement-set. As the agreement-set varies from one SPA to another, so the selection of a SPA will directly depends upon the gain obtained by SRA from the agreement-set of corresponding SPA. Hence, the IoS of a SRA with respect to a SPA will satisfy the following relation:

$$IoS \propto Gain(AgreementSet) \tag{5.1}$$

where, $Gain(AgreementSet)$ is the overall-gain of a SRA with respect to the reference SPA.

So, IoS of a SRA for a SPA can be defined as the weighted mean of the individual gains of the SRA for the various attributes involved in the negotiation between SRA and the corresponding SPA. Hence, IoS can be calculated as follows:

Let $A_1, A_2 \ldots A_n$ be the various attributes used for reaching the agreement in the negotiation process between SRA and a reference SPA. So, if $Gain(A_i)$ be the gain of SRA with respect to the reference SPA for the attribute A_i and W_i be the weightage given to the $Gain(A_i)$ in the calculation of IoS, then IoS can be represented by the following equation:

$$IoS = \frac{W_1 * Gain(A_1) + W_2 * Gain(A_2) + \ldots + W_n * Gain(A_n)}{W_1 + W_2 + \ldots + W_n} \tag{5.2}$$

OR

$$IoS = \frac{\sum\limits_{i=1}^{n} W_i * Gain(A_i)}{\sum\limits_{i=1}^{n} W_i} \tag{5.3}$$

Now, the calculation for $Gain(A_i)$ can be done as follows:

Various attributes of a service can have user-tendency of either 'lower the better' or 'higher the better'. For example, for the attribute such as price, lower the value of this attribute more favorable this will be to the requester, so it has user-tendency 'lower the better', while for the attribute such as quality, higher the value of this attribute more favorable this will be to the requester, so it has user-tendency 'higher the better'. Let out of the n number of attributes, $A_1, A_2 \ldots A_t, A_{t+1} \ldots A_n$, of a service, the t number of attributes, $A_1, A_2 \ldots A_t$, have the user-tendency 'lower the better' and the remaining $(n-t)$ number of attributes, $A_{t+1}, A_{t+2} \ldots A_n$, have the user-tendency 'higher the better'. Further consider that for the attribute set $(A_1, A_2 \ldots A_t, A_{t+1} \ldots A_n)$, the negotiation between the SRA and the reference SPA results into the agreement-set $(Vag_1, Vag_2 \ldots Vag_t, Vag_{t+1} \ldots Vag_n)$ and the expectation-set of SRA is $(Vex_1, Vex_2 \ldots Vex_t, Vex_{t+1} \ldots Vex_n)$. Then, the gain of SRA with reference to an individual attribute A_k can be defined as:

For $k = 1, 2, \ldots t$, the gain of SRA with reference to the attribute A_k can be defined by the value the agreed attribute-value, Vag_k, is lower than the expected attribute-value Vex_k and hence is represented by the Eq. (5.4). Similarly for $k = t+1, t+2, \ldots n$, the gain of SR with reference to the attribute A_k can be defined by the value the agreed attribute-value, Vag_k, is higher than the expected attribute-value Vex_k and hence is represented by the Eq. (5.5).

For

$$k = 1, 2, \ldots t \quad Gain(A_k) = \frac{Vex_k - Vag_k}{Vex_k} \tag{5.4}$$

For

$$k = t+1, t+2, \ldots n \quad Gain(A_k) = \frac{Vag_k - Vex_k}{Vag_k} \tag{5.5}$$

We can see that different attributes have different value-ranges, value-types and measurements. As was discussed, the user may have different tendencies towards different attributes. In addition, the attribute may have higher weight in calculation of IoS, but its impact may be lowered by its smaller value than other attributes. The above model solves these problems by presenting the normalization of attributes. Equations (5.4) and (5.5) provides the normalization using the denominators Vex_k and Vag_k such that gain-value of all attributes lie between 0 and 1. The numerators in Eqs. (5.4) and (5.5) generates the attribute-values such that all gain-values have the user-tendency 'higher the better'. Thus, the Eq. (5.3) can be given the following form:

$$IoS = \frac{\sum\limits_{i=1}^{t} W_i * Gain(A_i) + \sum\limits_{i=t+1}^{n} W_i * Gain(A_i)}{\sum\limits_{i=1}^{n} W_i} \qquad (5.6)$$

5.5 Evaluation

The evaluation and validation of proposed NACM and NASM have been presented in this section. For evaluating the presented service composition approach, NACM, the evaluation approach described in Feenstra et al. 2007 can be used. Feenstra et al. 2007 have presented an approach for evaluating Web service composition approaches. This can also be used to evaluate the composition features of SWS composition approaches. They have described four evaluation criteria for composition methods:

1. Does the method provide support for the multi-actor perspective?
2. Does the method provide the ability to express and evaluate non-functional requirements? Does the method still support the composition process when service properties are unknown?
3. Does the method provide insight into alternative compositions, for example, in the case a part of a composition fails?
4. Does the method support the planning or the creation of a shared view on the composition? For example, does it provide an overview of missing services, or services that have to be changed?

The details of these criteria can be referred from Feenstra et al. (2007).

For a composition process to support a multi-actor perspective, the decision regarding the composition of services should be taken within the network containing different actors and all actors should cooperate to realize a common high-level goal (Feenstra et al. 2007). In NACM, the decision of composition is taken by a selected coordinator agent available on the Web. Different decomposed tasks are performed by the various SPAs towards achieving a high-level goal of satisfying input-request. Thus, first criterion is satisfied.

NACM uses two mathematical models viz. CPBSM and NASM for formalizing various non-functional parameters. Further, in the service composition process the tasks which need to be performed for satisfying input composite-request are not pre-defined. But, these tasks are decided during the course of action. The provider services for each of the tasks are selected dynamically by evaluation using NASM. Thus, the second criterion is also satisfied.

The proposed composition model, NACM, uses the NASM to rank the various candidate SPAs based upon their negotiation-agreements. So, the insight into the alternative compositions can be easily provided. NASM calculates an index of selection for various SPAs and the SPA with most suitable agreement and hence the highest index is selected. But if the selected SPA fails, then the next SPA in the ranking with next suitable agreement can be invoked to perform the specified task. This enables the proposed model to also satisfy third criterion.

The proposed composition model also satisfies the fourth criterion of planning support. NACM, in addition to checking the desire of agent before performing selection using CPBSM, can also perform the selection of SPAs for different decomposed tasks in parallel using NASM. So, after the selection process is over, the realization of composition process can be easily checked. Thus, all the four criteria described in the benchmark for evaluation of service composition approaches by Feenstra et al. (2007) are satisfied by the presented composition model.

Further, the NACM has been evaluated by comparing it with existing similar works. Large numbers of SWS composition approaches have been presented in the literature. Some of them are (Gomez-Perez et al. 2004; Sell et al. 2004; Wu et al. 2003, 2006; Lecue and Leger 2005; Arpinar et al. 2004; Chen et al. 2003; Pistore et al. 2004; Agarwal et al. 2004; McIlraith and Son 2002; Kvaloy et al. 2005; Charif and Sabouret 2005; Cao et al. 2005; Kungas et al. 2004; Kungas and Matskin 2005; Preist et al. 2002). But, out of these only a few such as Cao et al. (2005), Kungas et al. (2004), Kungas and Matskin (2005), Preist et al. (2002) are there which have presented the negotiation-based SWS composition.

Cao et al. (2005) have proposed a workflow and agent enabled service composition, based upon multi-agent negotiation. They have proposed the methodology of modeling the service composition as a constraint satisfaction problem and have used the multi-agent negotiation algorithm for solving it. Mainly the aspects related to multi-agent negotiation involved in service composition system have been emphasized. But, a very limited discussion have been provided to the various processes in service composition such as discovery, selection etc. Further, no modeling for the service selection process was found.

Preist et al. (2002) have presented a web service composition approach for composition of e-services. They have performed the negotiation in the multiple auctions simultaneously with the customer as well as with the service providers to dynamically generate the composite service. But, they have mainly presented the various negotiation aspects for performing negotiation in multiple auctions simultaneously. A very limited discussion has been found on the selection and composition of services and no formalization for service selection has been presented.

The works by Kungas et al. (2004), and Kungas and Matskin (2005) have shown the use of symbolic negotiation for the discovery process in service composition. Kungas and Matskin (2005) have also presented the use of non-symbolic negotiation for negotiating over the cost or other such attributes of composite service. But, a very limited discussion on the service selection has been found.

Apart from the mentioned aspects, none of the described similar works discuss the architectural detail of service composition process. A very limited discussion on the service selection and composition has been provided by them with no

Table 5.1 Comparative evaluation of proposed composition model

Feature	SWS composition approach by Cao et al. 2005	SWS composition approach by Preist et al. 2002	SWS composition approach by Kungas et al. 2004	SWS composition approach by Kungas and Matskin 2005	Our proposed SWS composition approach
Negotiation-based service composition	Yes	Yes	Yes	Yes	Yes
Using negotiation-agreements in service selection	No	No	No	No	Yes
Providing architecture for a negotiation-based SWS composition system	No	No	No	No	Yes
Providing consideration to the SRA-gain from the agreement with a SPA, in selection of that SPA	No	No	No	No	Yes
Providing formalization for the calculation of negotiation-gain of SRA	No	No	No	No	Yes
Formalized modeling for the selection of SPA	No	No	No	No	Yes

formal modeling for service selection. Further, they have used negotiation as a supporting activity in the service composition process, but not as the basis of selection as in our proposed model. Thus, the proposed model for service selection and composition is more efficient model for negotiation-based SWS composition. The tabular comparison in Table 5.1, summarizing the comparison of our proposed SWS composition approach, NACM, with other similar works discussed previously, also supports this argument.

Similar to the attribute-gain values calculated in the NASM, the work by Zhang et al. (2005) have also provided the formulation for calculation of quality-gain, cost-gain, and duration-gain. Like our proposed model, this work also properly handles the user-tendency and generates the gain values with user-tendency 'higher the better' irrespective of the user-tendency of attribute. But, our formulation is better in the sense that it is more near to the human intuition. The gain values calculated by the Zhang et al. (2005) always lies between 0 and 1, so it will always indicate that the SRA has some gain irrespective that the corresponding SPA has agreed on value lower than the expected value or higher than the expected value. For example, if the expected quality is 30 and the agreed quality is 20, then actually it is losing, but the formulation by Zhang et al. (2005) will show the gain-value of 0.667 i.e. positive gains. On the other hand, our formulation will generate the negative gain-value of -0.5 indicating that the SRA is losing. This fact can be easily verified by the following calculation:

For this purpose, we have taken the test data from an example described in Zhang et al. (2005). They have used the following values of different parameters: required threshold for quality, cost, and duration is 50, 50, and 55 respectively and the achieved values for an intermediate proposal is 30, 30, and 27 for quality, cost, and duration respectively. Out of these parameters, quality has the user-tendency of 'higher the better' and rest of two have user-tendency of 'lower the better'. So, it can be observed from general human intuition that the SRA is losing in the case of quality by value 20 i.e. gain of -20 and is gaining in case of cost and duration by values 20 and 28 respectively. The quality-gain, cost-gain, and duration-gain calculated using the formulation by Zhang et al. (2005) result into values 0.6, 0.4, and 0.509 respectively. On the other hand, by using Eq. (5.5) of our proposed model, NASM, for calculation of quality-gain and using Eq. (5.4) for calculation of cost-gain and duration-gain results into values -0.667, 0.4, and 0.509 respectively for quality gain, cost-gain, and duration-gain respectively. It can observed from these values that the gain-values calculated using our proposed model is clearly indicating that the SRA is losing in the case of quality which is consistent with the actual situation. It can also be seen from the Fig. 5.2 that the nature of curve corresponding to the gain-values calculated using our proposed model is more similar to the curve generated using actual gain values than the curve generated by values calculated using formulation from Zhang et al. (2005). Hence the proposed selection model will result into more reliable results.

5.6 Implementation

In this section, we have dealt with the issues in the implementation of a SWS composition system based upon the proposed composition model. We have implemented a SWS composition system based on the NACM. The system uses CPBSM (Kumar and Mishra 2008b) and NASM for the selection of coordinator agent and SPAs respectively. The implemented composition system represents an education planner. Education planner is the system which can be used for planning the complete process of securing admission in some higher education program. It involves various activities such as counseling and preparation for entrance examination, choosing the appropriate institute, getting funds, completing admission formalities, and arranging transportation to join. Thus, it involves activities requiring expert-advice. So, a semantic web based system can be helpful in this regard.

The implemented system uses Jena (HP Labs Semantic Web Programme 2008) for the implementation of the profiles of both coordinator and other task-specific

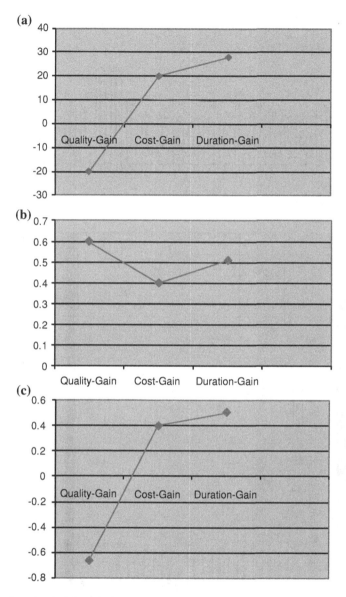

Fig. 5.2 **a** Actual gain-values, **b** Gain-values calculated using model from Zhang et al. (2005), **c** Gain-values calculated using our proposed model

agents in OWL (McGuinness and Harmelen 2008). These profiles are published on the web and can be accessed or manipulated by the SWS composition system. Structure of a profile prepared using Jena Ontology APIs and observed in Altova SemanticWorks (Altova 2008) for a SPA performing transportation-booking services is shown in Fig. 5.3. It can also be seen from the figure that the ontology

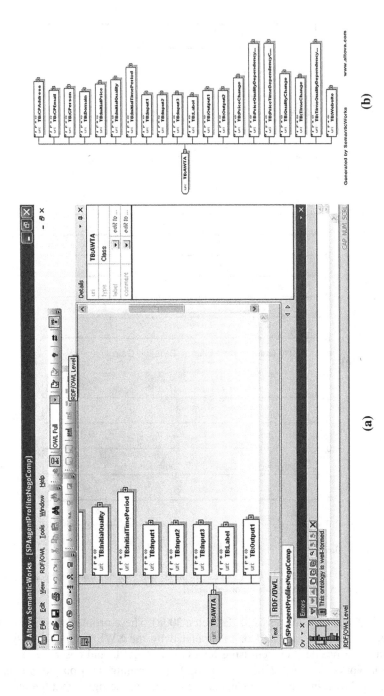

Fig. 5.3 a Transportation-booking agent profile, b Transportation-booking agent profile

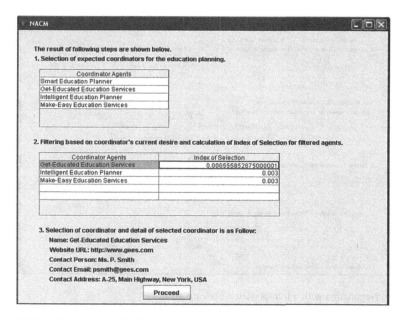

Fig. 5.4 Coordinator agent selection

in the profile is well-defined under OWL-Full RDF/OWL level. The system uses Jena's OWLReasoner for performing the inferencing in the system. Further, the composition system has been implemented using Java and related tools. This system easily access the OWL service profiles and uses the Jena APIs (Application Programming Interfaces) for manipulating, querying, or interrogating the service profiles. The querying support provided by Jena APIs is internally implemented in the SPARQL language (Prudhommeaux and Seaborne 2008). During the discovery of candidate SPAs, the exact-match approach of SWS matchmaking has been implemented.

The composition process starts with the input of composite input-ontology in the system. This ontology have three components: Qualification Input like course in which admission is sought, entrance examination score, qualifying examination score; Additional Admission Requirements like session of admission, date of birth, gender; and Preference and Constraints like finance needed or not, map needed or not, budget constraint, travel class constraint etc. After that, the selection of coordinator agent takes place. In this system, we have performed the selection of coordinator agent using our earlier selection model CPBSM, however it can be performed with any other required model also. The process for the agents' domain based filtering, and further steps of CPBSM are shown in the Fig. 5.4. As shown in the figure, the selected coordinator agent is 'Get-Educated Education Services (http://www.gees.com)'. After the coordinator agent has been selected, the further steps of the composition process are performed. Further, the selection of SPAs is performed for all simple tasks obtained from the decomposition of composite

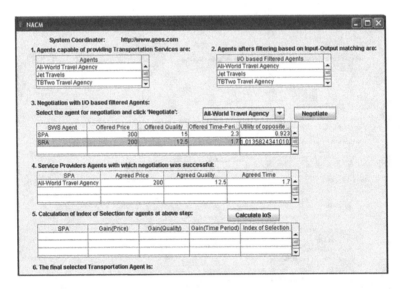

Fig. 5.5 Negotiation with a transportation-booking agent

request. It follows the process depicted in NACM involving validation of input, domain based filtering, IOPE filtering, negotiation with all the filtered SPAs and selection using NASM model.

Figure 5.5 shows the various steps of performing negotiation with a transportation-booking agent 'All-World Travel Agency' using a utility based multi-attribute negotiation approach (Kumar and Mishra 2009). At this step, the negotiation can be performed using any negotiation approach providing negotiation between SWSs.

The different steps of selecting a transportation-booking agent 'All-World Travel Agency' are shown in Fig. 5.6. First Table of Fig. 5.6 lists the agents after applying the domain based filtering. These are the available agents capable of providing transportation-booking services. Second table shows the agents obtained after applying input–output matching. Further, negotiation is performed with each of the filtered agents. The intermediate stages of the negotiation with an agent are shown in the third table. For an agent, if the negotiation at step 3 is successful, then the corresponding agreement is shown in the fourth table. So, fourth table shows all those SPAs with the corresponding agreements, with which the negotiation is successful. Fifth table in the figure shows process of calculation of IoS for the SPAs in fourth table using NASM. Second, third, and fourth column in the fifth table shows the values of gain in price, quality, and response-time calculated using the Eqs. (5.4), (5.5), and (5.4) respectively. Using these values, the final IoS is calculated for the SPAs using Eq. (5.4), which is shown in the last column of fifth table. It can be seen from the fifth table that the SPA 'All-World Travel Agency'

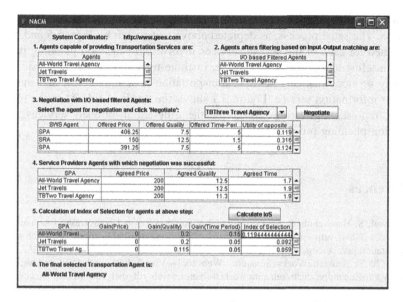

Fig. 5.6 Selection of transportation-booking agent

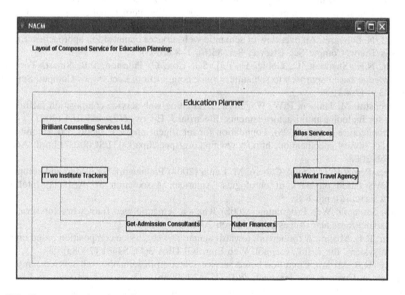

Fig. 5.7 Composed education planner

has highest IoS and hence it get selected as the provider for transportation-booking services. The same process, as depicted above and shown by Figs. 5.5 and 5.6, is performed for each of the simple services involved in education planning process i.e. counseling and preparation service, institute-tracking service, admission-consultancy service, financing service, transportation-booking service, and map and weather information service. Figure 5.7 shows the result of NACM in the form of blocks, representing various SPAs for the different mentioned services in the education planning process.

References

S. Agarwal, S. Handschuh, S. Staab, Annotation, composition and invocation of semantic web services (2004), http://www.uni-koblenz.de/ ~ staab/Research/Publications/2004/web-service-annotation.pdf. Accessed 26 March 2009

Altova (2008) SemanticWorks Semantic Web tool—Visual RDF and OWL editor, http://www.altova.com/products/semanticworks/semantic_web_rdf_owl_editor.html. Accessed 01 March 2008

I.B. Arpinar, B. Aleman-Meza, R. Zhang, A. Maduko, Ontology-Driven Web Services Composition Platform. In *Proceedings of IEEE International Conference on E- Commerce Technology, CEC'04*, (IEEE Press, San Diego, 2004), pp. 146–152

J. Cao, J. Wang, S. Zhang, M. Li, A multi-agent negotiation based service composition method for on demand service. In proceedings of the 2005 IEEE international conference on services computing (SCC'05). IEEE Comput. Soc. **1**, 329–332 (2005)

Y. Charif, N. Sabouret, An overview of semantic web services composition approaches. Electron. Notes Theor. Comput Sci. Elsevier Sci. **85**(6), 1–8 (2005)

L. Chen, N.R. Shadbolt, C. Goble, F. Tao, S.J. Cox, C. Puleston, P.R. Smart, Towards a knowledge-based approach to semantic service composition. Lect. Notes Comput. Sci. **2870**, 319–334 (2003)

R.W. Feenstra, M. Janssen, R.W. Wagenaar, Evaluating web service composition methods: the need for including multi-actor elements. Electron. J. E-Gov. **5**(2), 153–164 (2007)

FIPA Architecture Board (2008), Foundation for intelligent physical agents, FIPA communicative act library specification, http://www.fipa.org/specs/fipa00037/SC00037J.html. Accessed 12 Feb 2008

A. Gomez-Perez, R. Gonzalez-Cabero, M. Lama (2004) Framework for design and composition of SWS based on stack of ontologies. American Association for Artificial Intelligence (www.aaai.org), pp. 1–8

HP Labs Semantic Web Programme (2008) Jena—a semantic web framework for Java, http://jena.sourceforge.net/. Accessed 01 March 2008

S. Kumar, R.B. Mishra, A framework towards semantic web service composition based on multi-agent system. Int. J. Inf. Technol. Web Eng. IGI USA **3**(4), 59–81 (2008a)

S. Kumar, R.B. Mishra, Cognition based service selection in semantic web service composition models. J. Comput. Sci. Infocomp **7**(3), 35–42 (2008b)

S. Kumar, R.B. Mishra, An approach to multi-attribute negotiation between semantic web services. Int. J. Web Eng. Technol. **5**(2), 162–186 (2009)

P. Kungas, M. Matskin, *Combining Symbolic and Non-Symbolic Negotiation for Agent-Based Web Service Composition Proceedings of the 2005 International Conference on Artificial Intelligence ICAI'05* (CSREA Press, Las Vegas, 2005), pp. 513–519

P. Kungas, J. Rao, M. Matskin, Symbolic agent negotiation for semantic web service exploitation. Lect. Notes Comput. Sci. **3129**, 458–467 (2004)

T.A. Kvaloy, E. Rongen, A. Tirado-Ramos, P. Sloot, Automatic composition and selection of semantic web services. Lect. Notes Comput. Sci. **3470**, 184–192 (2005)

F. Lecue, A. Leger, A Formal Model for Semantic Web Service Composition. In *Proceedings of the 5th International Semantic Web Conference* (Athens, 2005)

M. Matskin, O.J. Kirkeluten, S.B. Krossnes, S. Sæle, *Agora: An Infrastructure For Cooperative Work Support In Multi-Agent Systems*, ed. by T. Wagner, O.F. Rana, International Workshop on Infrastructure for Multi-Agent Systems, Barcelona 2001. Lecture Notes in Computer Science, vol. 1887, (Springer-Verlag, 2001), pp. 28–40

D.L. McGuinness, F.V. Harmelen, OWL web ontology language overview (2008), http://www.w3.org/TR/owl-features/. Accessed 13 Feb 2008

S. McIlraith, T.C. Son, Adapting Golog for composition of semantic web services. *Proceedings of the Eighth International Conference on Knowledge Representation and Reasoning (KR2002)*, (Toulouse, 2002), pp. 482–493

M. Paolucci, T. Kawamura, T. Payne, K. Sycara, Semantic Matching of Web Service Capabilities. In *Proceedings of International Semantic Web Conference* (ISWC, 2002)

M. Pistore, P. Bertoli, E. Cusenza, A. Marconi, P. Traverso, *WS-GEN: A tool for the automated composition of semantic web services. Proceedings of the International Semantic Web Conference* (ISWC, 2004)

C. Preist, A. Byde, C. Bartolini, G. Piccinelli, Towards agent-based service composition through negotiation in multiple auctions. AISB J. **1**(1) (2002). http://www.aisb.org.uk

E. Prudhommeaux, A. Seaborne, SPARQL query language for RDF (2008). http://www.w3.org/TR/2008/REC-rdf-sparql-query-20080115/. Accessed 01 March 2008

D. Sell, F. Hakimpour, J. Domingue, E. Motta, R. Pacheco, Interactive composition of WSMO-based semantic web services in IRS-III. In *Proceedings of the AKT Workshop on Semantic Web Services (AKT-SWS04)*, (2004)

Smith and Davis (2008) Foundation for intelligent physical agents. FIPA contract net interaction protocol specification, http://www.fipa.org/specs/fipa00029/SC00029H.html. Accessed 12 Feb 2008

M. Stollberg, A. Haller, Semantic Web Services Tutorial. *Third International Conference on Web Services* (ICWS, 2005)

The DAML Services Coalition (2008) DAML-S: Semantic mark-up for web services, http://www.daml.org/services/daml-s/2001/10/daml-s.pdf. Accessed 13 Feb 2008

D. Wu, B. Parsia, E. Sirin, J. Hendler, D. Nau, Automating DAML-S Web Services Composition Using SHOP2. In *Proceedings of the 2nd International Semantic Web Conference (ISWC 2003)* (Sanibel Island, 2003)

Z. Wu, A. Ranabahu, K. Gomadam, A.P. Sheth, J.A. Miller, Automatic semantic web services composition (2006), www.cs.uga.edu/~jam/papers/zLSDISpapers/zixin.doc. Accessed 26 March 2009

X. Zhang, V. Lesser, R. Podorozhny, Multi-Dimensional, Multi-Step Negotiation for task Allocation in a Cooperative System. J. Auton. Ag. Multi-Ag. Syst **10**(1), 5–40 (2005)

About the Author

Sandeep Kumar is currently working as an Assistant Professor in the Electronics and Computer Engineering Department of the Indian Institute of Technology Roorkee (India). He has done his Ph.D. in Computer Engineering from the Indian Institute of Technology (Banaras Hindu University), Varanasi (India). In his course work for Ph.D., he has secured the highest possible grade of 'S' with ten out of ten CGPA. He was the Gold Medalist of Kurukshetra University in B.Tech. He has published more than 40 research papers, articles, and book chapters in various reputed international journals and conferences. He is the reviewer, editorial board member, and advisory committee member of various international journals and conferences. He is the member of board of examiners and board of studies of various universities and institutions. His biography has been listed by and he has been selected for various awards by different organizations such as Marquis Who's Who, International Biographical Centre Britain, American Biographical Institute USA. He is actively involved as the principal investigator in research project and is guiding various research students. His areas of interest include Semantic Web, Web Services, Multiagent systems, and Software Engineering. He can be contacted at sandeepkumargarg@gmail.com.

S. Kumar, *Agent-Based Semantic Web Service Composition*,
SpringerBriefs in Electrical and Computer Engineering,
DOI: 10.1007/978-1-4614-4663-7, © The Author(s) 2012